The

Year

of the

Poet VII

July 2020

The Poetry Posse

inner child press, ltd.

The Poetry Posse 2020

Gail Weston Shazor

Shareef Abdur Rasheed

Teresa E. Gallion

hülya n. yılmaz

Kimberly Burnham

Tzemin Ition Tsai

Elizabeth Esguerra Castillo

Jackie Davis Allen

Joe Paire

Caroline 'Ceri' Nazareno

Ashok K. Bhargava

Alicja Maria Kuberska

Swapna Behera

Albert 'Infinite' Carrasco

Eliza Segiet

William S. Peters, Sr.

~ * ~

In order to maintain each poet's authentic voice, this volume has not undergone the scrutiny of editing. Please take time to indulge each contributor for their own creativity and aspirations to convey their uniqueness.

hülya n. yılmaz, Ph.D.
Director of Editing ~
Inner Child Press International

General Information

The Year of the Poet VII
July 2020 Edition

The Poetry Posse

1ˢᵗ Edition : 2020

Publisher Information
1ˢᵗ Edition : Inner Child Press
intouch@innerchildpress.com
www.innerchildpress.com

ISBN-13 : 978-1-952081-22-4 (inner child press, ltd.)

$ 12.99

WHAT WOULD LIFE BE WITHOUT A LITTLE POETRY?

Dedication

This Book is dedicated to

Humanity, Peace & Poetry

the Power of the Pen

can effectuate change!

&

The Poetry Posse

past, present & future

our Patrons and Readers

the Spirit of our Everlasting Muse

In the darkness of my life
I heard the music
I danced . . .
and the Light appeared
and I dance

Janet P. Caldwell

Table of Contents

Foreword   *ix*

Preface   *xi*

Norman E. Borlaug   *xv*

The Poetry Posse

Gail Weston Shazor   1

Alicja Maria Kuberska   9

Jackie Davis Allen   13

Tezmin Ition Tsai   21

Shareef Abdur – Rasheed   27

Kimberly Burnham   35

Elizabeth Esguerra Castillo   41

Joe Paire   49

hülya n. yılmaz   57

Teresa E. Gallion   65

Table of Contents . . . *continued*

Ashok K. Bhargava   71

Caroline Nazareno-Gabis   77

Swapna Behera   83

Albert Carassco   91

Eliza Segiet   97

William S. Peters, Sr.   103

July's Featured Poets   115

Mykola Martyniuk   117

Orbindu Ganga   125

Roula Pollard   131

Karn Praktisha   137

Inner Child News   145

Other Anthological Works   173

Foreword

Welcome to the 79th volume of *The Year of the Poet* brought to you by the Inner Child Press Poetry Posse plus a few featured friends. Within the microcosm of peace and Nobel Peace Prize winners, this month we turn our attention to sustainability, a green revolution that has been building for a long time. We amplify the voice of one man who wanted to see each person feed. We ask ourselves how we can help sustain the world, not just those who are rich, those who are in urban environments, or just those in rural farms, and we are still looking for answers 79 or so years after Norman Borlaug started helping Mexico become self-sufficient in wheat. An American born in 1914, Borlaug won the 1970 Nobel Peace Prize. His goal was to strike a balance between population growth and food production—creating enough food to sustain everyone's dreams and ambitions. Borlaug's success in Mexico made him a much sought-after adviser especially in South American and Asian countries where food production was not keeping pace with population growth.

As poets we use our creativity, awareness, and pens to bring both peace and sustainability to the world. With enough creativity to find solutions that have been overlooked, spreading the word about the possibility for greatness in a world where every child is nourished, we bringing consciousness through sharing our thoughts, listening to those around us, and reflecting back our community wisdom. In a diverse environment many great ideas can thrive, grow, and be amplified by those who listen and see the beauty in diversity and sustainability for all. A pen, a computer, letters on a sheet of paper, we say are mightier than the sword. We lay down our swords to write, think and pray for a spark that will ignite a generation bringing peace and justice to the darkness.

Peace can grow and hunger subside when each person's contribution matters, is seen and valued. As you read these poems listen to the cacophony of voices they represent, not because we few are representative of all but because we each grow in different environments, learn unusual things and listen to those in our diverse communities. Our words reflect our love of one person, a community, the natural world, or an idea. As we put pen to paper or fingers to the keyboard, we seek to create a world in which each voice is valued, and each person is nurtured.

All this while, still realizing that we live in a world where we have the power to amplify certain voices and affirm: Black Lives Matter.

Kimberly Burnham,
Spokane, WA

Preface

Dear Family and Friends,

Yes I am excited and feel accomplished as we enter our seventh year of publishing what I and many others deem to be a worthy enterprise, *The Year of the Poet*.

This past year we have aligned our vision with that of Nober Peace Prize Recipients. We have title this year's theme. The Year of Peace! Hopefully thorugh our sharing each month, our poetry can have a profound effect on our global consciousness and the need for peace while educating ourselves and our readership about some of the individuals who have made history through their efforts to promulgate peace for all of humanity.. We are on our way to hitting yet another milestone. Needless to say, I am elated.

To reiterate, our initial vision was to just perform at this level for the year of 2014. Since that time we have had the blessed opportunity to include many other wonderful poets, word artists and storytellers in the Poetry Posse from lands, cultures and persuasions all over the world. We have featured hundreds of additional poets, thereby introducing their poetic offerings to our vast global audience.

In keeping with our effort and vision to expand the awareness of poets from all walks by making this offerings accessible, we at Inner Child Press International will continue to make every volume a FREE Download. The books are also available for purchase at the affordable cost of $7.00 per volume.

In the previous years, our monthly themes were Flowers, Birds, Gemstones, Trees and Past Cultures. This coming year we have elected to continue our focus of choosing what we consider a significant subject . . . PEACE! In each month's volume you will have the opportunity to not only read at least one poem themed by our Poetry Posse members about such celebrated Peace Ambassadors, but we have included a few words about each individual in our prologue. We hope you find the poetic offerings insightful as we use our poetic form to relay to you what we too have learned through our research in making our offering available to you, our readership.

In closing, we would like to thank you for being an integral part of our amazing journey.

Enjoy our amazing featured poets . . . they are amazing!

Building Cultural Bridges of Understanding . . .

Bless Up . . . From the home in our hearts to yours

Bill

The Poetry Posse
Inner Child Press Ineternational

PS

Do Not forget about the World Healing, World Peace Poetry effort.

Available here

www.worldhealingworldpeacepoetry.com

**For Free Downloads of Previous Issues of
The Year of the Poet**

www.innerchildpress.com/the-year-of-the-poet

World Healing World Peace
2020

Poets for Humanity

Now Available

www.innerchildpress.com/world-healing-world-peace-poetry

www.worldhealingworldpeacepoetry.com

www.worldhealingworldpeacefoundation.org

Norman E. Borlaug
1970

Each month for the year of 2020, which we have deemed as *The Year of Peace*, we at Inner Child Press International will be celebrating through our poetry a few Nobel Peace Prize Recipients who have contributed greatly to humanity via their particular avocations. This month of Julu 2020 you will find select poems from each Poetry Posse member on this month's celebrants.

In 1970, The Nobel Peace Prize was awarded to Norman E. Borlaug.

For more information about visit :

en.wikipedia.org/wiki/Norman_Borlaug
or
www.nobelprize.org/prizes/peace/1970/borlaug/bi ographical/

World Healing, World Peace Foundation
human beings for humanity

worldhealingworldpeacefoundation.org

xvi

Poets . . .
sowing seeds in the
Conscious Garden of Life,
that those who have yet to come
may enjoy the Flowers.

Poets, Writers . . . know that we are the enchanting magicians that nourishes the seeds of dreams and thoughts . . . it is our words that entice the hearts and minds of others to believe there is something grand about the possibilities that life has to offer and our words tease it forth into action . . . for you are the Poet, the Writer to whom the Gift of Words has been entrusted . . .

~ wsp

poetry is . . .

Poetry succeeds where instruction fails.

~ wsp

I Fly

because I Can

...said the Dreamer to the world.

Gail Weston Shazor

Gail Weston Shazor

This is a creative promise ~ my pen will speak to and for the world. Enamored with letters and respectful of their power, I have been writing for most of my life. A mother, daughter, sister and grandmother I give what I have been given, greatfilledly.

Author of . . .

"An Overstanding of an Imperfect Love"
&
Notes from the Blue Roof

Lies My Grandfathers Told Me

available at Inner Child Press.

www.facebook.com/gailwestonshazor
www.innerchildpress.com/gail-weston-shazor
navypoet1@gmail.com

Words Over Water

Civilization as it is known today could not have evolved,
nor can it survive, without an adequate food supply.

Speaking those words over the water
Help me heal mother earth
Give me the ways
For all reasons
To bring your life to the people on this soil
Ache us to listen
So that we may remember your ways

We have always been a people of reaping
So our color is so
Dark of the earth
Brought from the soil
Made of seed
Cracked in the despair
Of infinite birth

To call us civilization
Is at best, a lie
Please mother, show us
Something more than destruction
As we learn to be civil to you
Teach us once again
To love you
As you love us.

Sickness

I am writing
Between every wheeze and cough
On the edges of my breath
Sometimes the thought seeps
Out in my sleep between parted lips
And noisy snores
I hear my words trying to catch up
With the images in my head
That tread pillow to pillow

I can't breathe
I turn incessantly in my
Empty fishbowl
The fear and sweat pores
Stain my radiance
Into a tangle of raven wings
Blackened
As I imagine the whispers
Of what I want to say
Caught in my throat

I can't sleep
Drug induced wakings
Scatter my heartbeats
Pounding in my ears
Often mimicking a burglar
Or the neighbors walking
In the apartment next door
Banging
On their own risers

I am in pain
And I fail to find the words
That will explain to you
Just how this feels
This
Can't breathing
Can't sleeping
And hurting with every breath
With every movement
Carefully

I am waiting
For sleep to come
And the rest to happen
The breathing to become deep
I want to dream easy
Without the need for the
Water glass
I keep by my bed
To drown my coughs

Remember

Remember

Dismembered

Commemorated

Enshrinement

Retrospectment

Revivement

Conjuring

Memorializement

Alicja Maria Kuberska

Alicja Maria Kuberska – awarded Polish poetess, novelist, journalist, editor. She was born in 1960, in Świebodzin, Poland. She now lives in Inowrocław, Poland.

In 2011 she published her first volume of poems entitled: "The Glass Reality". Her second volume "Analysis of Feelings", was published in 2012. The third collection "Moments" was published in English in 2014, both in Poland and in the USA. In 2014, she also published the novel - "Virtual roses" and volume of poems "On the border of dream". Next year her volume entitled "Girl in the Mirror" was published in the UK and "Love me" , " (Not)my poem" in the USA. In 2015 she also edited anthology entitled "The Other Side of the Screen".

In 2016 she edited two volumes: "Taste of Love" (USA), "Thief of Dreams" (Poland) and international anthology entitled " Love is like Air" (USA). In 2017 she published volume entitled "View from the window" (Poland). She also edits series of anthologies entitled "Metaphor of Contemporary" (Poland)

Her poems have been published in numerous anthologies and magazines in Poland, the USA, the UK, Albania, Belgium, Chile, Spain, Israel, Canada, India, Italy, Uzbekistan, Czech Republic, South Korea and Australia. She was a featured poet of New Mirage Journal (USA) in the summer of 2011.

Alicja Kuberska is a member of the Polish Writers Associations in Warsaw, Poland and IWA Bogdani, Albania. She is also a member of directors' board of Soflay Literature Foundation.

History like a fairy tale
A poem dedicated to Norman E. Borlaug

The wheat queen set out to conquer the world.
She threw a golden coat of ears over her shoulders.
and she tucked red poppies,
and cornflowers in her light hair.
On the banners there were words
"green revolution".

A powerful army conquered fields and countries.
The wind, the ruler's silent ally,
sang joyfully about victory over hunger
and sprayed yellow pollen in the air like fireworks,
that it would smell of bread and hope

Scientist in the comfort of his laboratory
did a miracle to create a new species.
He hid the vital forces In inconspicuous grains
to provide rich crops to humanity

Abundance and satiety prevailed in the world.
One man - a modern hero
saved more lives from death
than anyone else before him

Stigmatized by hatred

They declare the glory of death loudly
and walk in puddles of blood.
Wrapped in bands of dynamite,
they believe
 they will soar to the gates of paradise.

Someone persuaded them
that contempt for life is sacred.
They depart,
assisted by the brutally murdered,
burdened with tears like a curse.

God separates
victims from executioners.

Wislawa Szymborska

We have not met in person.
She takes pride of place in my living room,
on the autographed photograph.
She is looking at me now
with playful, twinkling eyes.

I have got her volumes.
She is discrete in the silence of the plants
as she confides to a swallow about love.
The ringing phone is in her dreams
and she wanders around the children's cemetery.
I can see her standing
among the people on the bridge.

We see each other every day.
She speaks to me
in the words of her poems
as I meander through her poetry.

She left and stayed.
Everything can be forever.
I read the letters of her poetical mail
and I can hear her voiceless laughter

Jackie Davis Allen

Jackie Davis Allen, otherwise known as Jacqueline D. Allen or Jackie Allen, grew up in the Cumberland Mountains of Appalachia. As the next eldest daughter of a coal miner father and a stay at home mother, she was the first in her family to attend and graduate from college. Her siblings, in their own right, are accomplished, though she is the only one, to date, that has discovered the gift of writing.

Graduating from Radford University, with a Bachelors of Science degree in Early Education, she taught in both public and private schools. For over a decade she taught private art classes to children both in her home and at a local Art and Framing Shop where she also sold her original soft sculptured Victorian dolls and original christening gowns.

She resides in northern Virginia with her husband, taking much needed get-aways to their mountain home near the Blue Ridge Mountains, a place that evokes memories of days spent growing up in the Appalachian Mountains.

A lover of hats, she has worn many. Following marriage to her college sweetheart, and as wife, mother, grandmother, teacher, tutor, artist, writer, poet and crafter, she is a lover of art and antiques, surrounding herself, always, with books, seeking to learn more.

In 2015 she authored *Looking for Rainbows, Poetry, Prose and Art*, and in 2017, *Dark Side of the Moon*. Both books of mostly narrative poetry were published by Inner Child Press and were edited by hulya n. yilmaz.

in 2019, No Illusions.Through the Looking Glass, which was nominated to be considered for a Pulitzer Prize by the publisher and editor of InnerChild Press, ltd.

http://www.innerchildpress.com/jackie-davis-allen.php
jackiedavisallen.com

In the Name of Hunger

From a young farm boy,
To later, a bright shining star,
Somehow, Norman E. Borlaug knew.
        Knew that from determination's persistence,
           The diligent pursuit of education
             Would take him far.

From hunger of knowledge
To acquisition of interest's same,
Norman E Borlaug found a way.
        A way to increase wheat's production.
        The genetic modification's solution
        Spread wide and far, across the land.

From countries in dire straits' hunger
To elevated academic-fame, acclaim came.
From heart's desire, in 1970, awarded for his efforts,
        Norman E. Borlaug was awarded
      The Nobel Peace Prize. Lush wheat fields,
        Whispering, still, remember his name.

Confessional: As Is Her Right

On fence post, on guard,
sits a bird a mother-to-be.
Smell the fresh air, where
Beneath the indulgent blue
Not a cloud may be seen sailing by

Fat are the lilac buds, unfurled;
Standing near by, a host of daffodils.
And waiting in the wings,
alert, a little bird, leaning
neither left nor right.

The silence is broken;
hear her plaintive cry.
Do not disturb her little nest!
Cautioning any and all, she threatens
To dive-bomb those who would try.

The Loving-Tree

When mornings are born each day, and anew,
And skies are painted a crystal-clear, robin's egg blue,
The sun dances and kisses with hot lip's breeze,
The shoulders of the Loving-Tree.

A canopy of inciting passion blooms flowers.
Sweetly perfumed with honeyed scent
Of romance. Beneath the branches, love makes
A path. And in its all-knowing, leaves footprints.

When shadows of dissension fall dark
On the shoulders of the Loving-Tree,
Amid suspicion, or shades of dread, they dare to paint
Rejection's countenance with fear of revenge.

Should not love, then, bend in time with the weather?
As young saplings do? If they are to survive?
Should not lovers then take time to brave the tempest?
Should not love have a chance to grow anew?

The canopy of the Loving-Tree blooms flowers.
Flowers, sweetly perfumed with honeyed scent
Of romance. Beneath its branches, love makes a path.
And in its knowing leaves footprints.

Tzemin Ition Tsai

Dr. Tzemin Ition Tsai (蔡澤民博士) was born in Republic of China, in 1957. He holds a Ph.D. in Chemical Engineering and two Masters of Science in Applied Mathematics and Chemical Engineering. He is a professor at Asia University (Taiwan), editor of "Reading, Writing and Teaching" academic text. He also writes the long-term columns for Chinese Language Monthly in Taiwan.

He is a scholar with a wide range of expertise, while maintaining a common and positive interest in science, engineering and literature member. He is also an editor of "Reading, Writing and Teaching" academic text and a columnist for *'Chinese Language Monthly'* in Taiwan

He has won many national literary awards. His literary works have been anthologized and published in books, journals, and newspapers in more than 40 countries and have been translated into more than a dozen languages.

Dwarfing, The Later Role

Pain is going to pass
In its name
Not in its name
Many of the people who worked hard were starving
How foods changed their blood
All of this
Left scars on him

Semi-dwarf wheat.
When the days were getting shorter
In the north, were planting, at low elevation and high
temperature
Take the best seed south
When days were getting longer
There was lots of rain
Soon we had varieties that fit the whole range of conditions

Selecting an individual
A hungry world symbolizing agriculture and food
Both for bread and for peace
Whether by genetic modification or for freedom from
hunger
Most people still fail to comprehend the population
Monster
This is convincing or the whole thing was a hoax
Oh, Pain is going to pass
In its name
Not in its name

Smile In Heart For The Smiling Flower

That drizzle always a misty white
My husband accompanied with a smile hide under an
umbrella
Losing part of bold and straightforward of being young
Only laughed at me gently
You are a nerd
The smiling flowers inside others' walls
Unexpectedly, more real than that psychological thoughts
lay at your heart
You came so often and stop here
Begging the owner who came to answer the door
Allowed to pick several flowers
Through the breeze blowing
This old book
Paging through the page that have been pressed countless
times
That mottled imprints
Accepted my request without a word
Eager heart
Before patience was exhausted
Pressed flowers made of smiling flowers
Keep all the fragrance with the envelope
Sent to my son thousands of miles away
The smiley flower that endured the pain still smiled
Seems, it understands
This spring let me
How grieved?

Chanting For Falling Flowers

There was a long time
I thought that poem
Just to show gorgeous
Or just to show good qualities
Better than
The bright moon at night

There was a long time
I thought that poem
Just to help others laugh
Or just to suppress the sadness of parting
Dispatching the loyalty of emotions
Made the evil spirits and the gods sad

Great conjecture, since
Only I understood in the world
Your thin and beautiful frame
Was as pretty as the poignant beauty of plum blossoms
Only you knew in the world
I have looked the messages in poetry lighter and lighter
No longer complaining that the good-looking was so easy
to die away
Beyond this mortal world
Why, I
Needed to hold up this black nib
Created all this endless spring, boundless thinking

Shareef
Abdur
Rasheed

Shareef Abdur Rasheed

Shareef Abdur-Rasheed, AKA Zakir Flo was born and raised in Brooklyn, New York. His education includes Brooklyn College, Suffolk County Community College and Makkah, Saudi Arabia. He is a Veteran of the Viet Nam era, where in 1969 he reverted to his now reverently embraced Islamic Faith. He is very active in the Islamic community and beyond with his teachings, activism and his humanity.

Shareef's spiritual expression comes through the persona of "Zakir Flo" . Zakir is Arabic for "To remind". Never silent, Shareef Abdur-Rasheed is always dropping science, love, consciousness and signs of the time in rhyme.

Shareef is the Patriarch of the Abdur-Rasheed Family with 9 Children (6 Sons and 3 Daughters) and 41 Grandchildren (24 Boys and 17 Girls).

For more information about Shareef, visit his personal FaceBook Page at :

https://www.facebook.com/shareef.abdurrasheed1
https://zakirflo.wordpress.com

Norman Borlaug
born to feed humanity

immediately
occurred to me
Norman Borlaug
was born to feed
humanity
dedicated almost
entirely lifetime study
produce food
feed humanity
scientist of Agronomy
plant pathology, genetics
saw mankind pathetic
many millions starving,
dying
decided the need
supplying grains, wheat
to feed globally
increased opportunity
for wars to cease
increase the peace
shut down savage beast
starvation kills at will
feasts on corpses
until it's fat, full
Borlaug gave his life's
work to change that
Nobel Peace Prize
recipient 1970
supplied food for humanity
fact indeed
instrumental saving billions

food4thought = education

Virtue..,

where are you
seems your hiding
while millions dying
devils applying
deadly measures
permeate landscapes
motives born of hate
ignorance, evil dominates
north, south, west, east
controlled by beast
do not possess the least
amount of qualities
virtue reduced to concepts
abstract
almost extinct language
to be exact
few eyes see
much less what hearts
beat too
virtue equals
honor, loyalty,
honesty, consistency
upholding responsibility
reliability, dependability
almost nowhere does
god fear appears
to be seen
maybe rarely if any
words ain't worth a penny
bull$#!+ a plenty
this world seems empty

thus, what is prognosis
terminal at best?
mankind flunked the smell
test
yet goodness still in
some of us
and thee creator exist in
full effect
will fulfil his promise
thus, begin to correct
no doubt about
stay tuned, remain
on the look out

food4thought = education

presence of..,

evidence at crime scene
some seen some unseen
was it traces of blood
semen, fingerprints
rounds spent, hair
shoe prints, nails?
no none of that
instead..,
dignity, respect, family,
unity, morals, god fear
somebody was here
this isn't natural
straight up homicide
" death by deprivation "
said the M,E. who did
the autopsy
bled out large amounts
of trust, peace, security
due to over abundance
of hate, inhuman assault
denial of god given rights
life drained out
there seems to be a serial
killer out and about
stalking, stoking
flames designed
to kill and maim
especially people's
of african descent
until not a one remains
it's not enough that they were

brought here in chains
stripped of identity, language,
culture, religion, name
endure over 400 years of'
inflicted pain
epitome of all deemed
inhumane
until this second remains
as the innocent still
killed at will
deprived, slain
all in jesus name

food4thought = education

Kimberly Burnham

A brain health expert with a PhD in Integrative Medicine, Kimberly Burnham has lived in tropical Colombia; in Belgium during the Vietnam War; in Japan teaching businessmen English; in diverse international Toronto, Canada and several places in the US. Now, she's in Spokane, WA with her wife, Elizabeth, two sets of twins (age 11 & 14) and three dogs. Her recent book, *Awakenings: Peace Dictionary, Language and the Mind, a Daily Brain Health Program* includes the word for peace in hundreds of languages. Kim's poetry weaves through 70 volumes of *The Year of the Poet, Inspired by Gandhi, Women Building the World, A Woman's Place in the Dictionary*, Tiferet Journal, Human/Kind Journal and more.

https://www.nervewhisperer.solutions/
https://www.linkedin.com/in/kimberlyburnham/

Peace and Sustainability Begins With You

In Kaqchikel
an indigenous language of Mexico
and the Guatemalan highlands
peace begins with U
said "uxlanibel c'u'x"
literally "rest of the heart"

"Cukul -c'u'x" is translated calm
confident and faith
and I wonder which comes first
faith, confidence or calmness
or perhaps in a unique swirl of synchronicity
all three arrive together with good health
"cukul vachaj"

While "cukuba' vachaj" is to cheer up
and I consider the relationship between
health and happiness
the place where we meet
when the heart is at rest
and great lives are sustainable

Sparks of Life Unite

A spark of fire in the eyes of an activist
lights the way

In the heart of a grandmother
holding her first grandson

Feeding the belly of an entrepreneur
trying to create a future for his family

As a child learns about Norman E. Borlaug
a green revolution paves the way to a Nobel Peace Prize
and plenty

United we sparks
are enough to light the darkness

Forming a world warm and welcoming
for all bellies, hearts and minds satisfied

Pleasant Taste of Peace

In a Mayan language of the Yucatan peninsula
"Ci" or "Cici" means pleasant and agreeable
originally "what is pleasant to taste"

"Ol" is the mind, intention or will
while peace is "ciciol" also joy, pleasure
and happiness from "cici" and "ol"

As if when we have the pleasant taste of peace
we are agreeable and happy
life is a pleasure joy surrounds us

And we feel "Cicithan" words of love or a blessing
from "cici" and "than" words
may we all be blessed to savor the pleasant taste of peace

Elizabeth E. Castillo

Elizabeth Esguerra Castillo is a multi-awarded and an Internationally-Published Contemporary Author/Poet and a Professional Writer / Creative Writer / Feature Writer / Journalist / Travel Writer from the Philippines. She has 2 published books, "Seasons of Emotions" (UK) and "Inner Reflections of the Muse", (USA). Elizabeth is also a co-author to more than 60 international anthologies in the USA, Canada, UK, Romania, India. She is a Contributing Editor of Inner Child Magazine, USA and an Advisory Board Member of Reflection Magazine, an international literary magazine. She is a member of the American Authors Association (AAA) and PEN International.

Web links:

Facebook Fan Page

https://free.facebook.com/ElizabethEsguerraCastillo

Google Plus

https://plus.google.com/u/0/+ElizabethCastillo

The Man Who Saved Lives

In a starving and ailing world

Along came a noble man,

The hero of a billion lives

The Father of the "Green Revolution"

Must not forget his valuable contribution

Dedicated his entire life

To feed the hungry,

Let us not ever forget

The Man Who Saved a Billion Lives.

It's just once in a lifetime a real hero arrives

Bourlaug, the Man Who Fed the World.

Courage to be True

Do you have to hide your true self?
Make pretensions, be under disguise?
To be noticed by others, do you have to lie?
Look yourself in the mirror and ask yourself why?
Has the world made a slave out of you
That once you feel unappreciated,
You succumb to being blue?

In reality, those who don a mask,
Are the ones who don't know authentic happiness
For out of the mundane things, their joy dwells.
Living each day in their own make-believe world,
Lost souls, restless hearts, crying for freedom
To break free from the chains that bind
And to have the courage to be true to mankind.

Clowns are sent to entertain the crowd,
But beneath the thick layers of hues
Can we say that their smiles are true?
The funny comedian in the movies that we see
In real life emerges a depressed soul once alone
For behind the laughter, behind the cheer,
We can't see their real selves, can't see the hidden fear.

True, happy people don't have to mask their true selves,
For they don't seek validation or appreciation from others,
Simply by being their own self, being honest to what they
feel,
Open doors of love and acceptance for those who truly
care.

The Invisible Thread

I'm your first baby,
Always remain to be a little girl of my Daddy
You sheltered me under your strong wings,
Protected me from harm
With a solemn prayer
Each time I leave your side.

Even when I grew older
You still haven't outgrown treating me like a little girl,
I look up to you with such glorious respect
For you are a once in a lifetime Dad
We will never ever forget.

This invisible thread that connects us
They cannot decipher,
Maybe even if I'll be counting years
Your serene face in my mind
Still can vividly remember.

In the heavens I know
You were welcomed by Grandpa and Grandma,
With such a warm embrace
Upon entering its Holy gates.

You like telling fond memories of your childhood
As me and my sister lie on bed with you
Every afternoon when we we're still kids,
Your kind of music still lingers on
And your thoughtful love for us
We would truly miss.

You may have suffered in silence
Kept the pain just inside you
Worrying still about us
And even in your death bed
Your love for us you still showed.

The invisible thread that connects
The souls of a father and his daughter
Is truly special nothing can ever replace
For even if you're at the other side
I still can feel your comforting touch
Each time I shed tears missing you.

Joe
Paire

Joe Paire

Joseph L Paire' aka Joe DaVerbal Minddancer . . .
is a quiet man, born in a time where civil liberties
were a walk on thin ice. He's been a victim of his
own shyness often sidelined in his own quest for
love. He became the observer, charting life's path.
Taking note of the why, people do what they do. His
writings oft times strike a cord with the
dormant strings of the reader. His pen the rosined
bow drawn across the mind. He comes full-frontal
or in the subtlest way, always expressing in a way
that stimulate the senses.

www.facebook.com/joe.minddancer

Plant Man

Norman Ernest Borlaug could see
the benefit of growing strong wheat
"Academic butterflies" need not apply
For the focus of it all, is so people can eat

Population explosions take tolls and defuse the idea
The method of growth was made quite clear
It's so hard to adhere and appear to be ethical
Norman held fast, and his crops were exceptional

Peace through cereal grains, cease through material gains
Profits never profit on an ethereal plain
Norman got down in the dirt with his fellow man
There's a street named somewhere in honor of him

Bread and water for basic sustenance
Why not enhance the yield for the populous
Thriving metropolis to surviving apocalypse
Norman cared enough and continued to stay on top of it

Nobel peace prize winner, there's even bicker over food
Who knew what wars were brewed over mead?
Who stewed over seeds, who produced over greed?
Teach them to be self-sufficient, it's ammunition

Norman Ernest Borlaug could see
the benefit of growing strong wheat
"Academic butterflies" need not apply
For the focus of it all, is so people can eat

Pacified

I've seen the news and been behind the scenes
People are being saddled and bridled
As life is supposed to be, as opposed to free
"They shoot horses don't they"
So why won't they kill a "Trigger"
"Hi Ho Silver" to Jay Silver's Kemosabe
it's okay to rob me, pacify through policy
Spend crumbs on an apology never applied
Much less implied, more like implicated
Human element totally vacated
The constitution say's its like that and that's the way it is
Shackled like cattle from majority fears
it's never cool, to do the right things
The rules are to act like who would be king.
King of the block, Best at what's best at
Where does it stop? I can only question the end

I've seen the news and been behind the scenes
I've been pronounced guilty for a crime I didn't commit
Change of policy after no apology
Just another loophole for the celebrated noose hold
No ban on the choke hold for its they; that seek a pacifier
I seem to be important now
my needs are not distorted now,
it's always been about respect but WOW!
I know I'm not martyr material
Abolishing symbols and constant reminders
just how far behind we are on a "Level playing field"
if we shovel like we did, no questions asked
because we better not ask, arranged fruit
or remain mute, the square root of uppity is?
Don't pacify me while I question this.

Joe Paire

I don't wrestle with the obvious I have no job in this
No place in a society whose sobriety is to hate me
Belittle, undermine and berate me
Census take me for a number
of how many crumbs to spend, while cronies need only
be a host now and then, so proud within the margins
Blackout the Senate bargains, no point in arguing what
Barr gains, law games with jargon to jettison a pardon
let us get up on them, who juggle with the truth
While struggling with the proof,
there's a blackline through it
only a judge's eyes, now who's stupid?
When will the voters will be law?
When the voters quill these laws
It's true the rules are flawed but pacify me oh lord
I can't dance today.

I Miss Me

Every year was the same
I could watch time go by as easy as
Counting sunsets
I knew before the trees what a winter this would be
An eclipse was soon to happen
I stood on the wrong side of the moon
I won't be doing anything this summer

My collection is growing, I must sell my repeats
I suffer from what is known as, yet I'm so discrete
Bone in teeth never let's go, I've never said let's go
So, she took me for a ride, I miss me saying so
I'd wish we stayed at home
Everything ain't for everybody
I knew before the trees what a winter this would be

Duplicity or duplicated, I must sell my repeats
For the archeologist among you
I'm trying to stop my bad deeds
improve some sad things I never do anything
Just to wet my feet.
addictive behavior is not predictive behavior
I took the long way home.

Joe Paire

hülya

n.

yılmaz

hülya n. yılmaz

Liberal Arts Emerita, hülya n. yılmaz is a published author, literary translator, and Co-Chair and Director of Editing Services at Inner Child Press International. Her poetic work appeared in an excess of eighty-five anthologies of global endeavors and has been presented at numerous national and international poetry events. In 2018, the Writer's International Network of British Colombia, Canada honored yılmaz with a literary award. As of 2017, two of her poems remain permanently installed in *Telepoem Booth* – a U.S.-wide poetic art exhibition. hülya finds it vital for everyone to understand a deeper sense of self, and writes creatively to attain a comprehensive awareness for and development of our humanity.

Writing Web Site
https://hulyanyilmaz.com/

Editing Web Site
https://hulyasfreelancing.com

can you imagine?

you live to be 79
two years before your death
a Nobel Peace Prize is awarded to you

many an outstanding achievement stand by
all to your credit as a highly notable scientist
your accomplishments in the field of agriculture
remain for generations in the public eye

not only have you founded The World Food Prize
but have worked throughout your adult life
to feed the hungry globally

you have persevered in your tireless efforts
to integrate your field's numerous research branches
into sustainable technologies to nourish the world,
never wavering from your efforts
to convince political leaders
that the fruits of the advances
you had introduced all over the globe
needed to be harvested properly
for the sake of the entirety of humanity

the war you fought against
has not been one of weaponry
you have instead battled persistently
for food to ensure the survival of all
not only in your own country
but rather all-inclusively

then . . .

as imagination would and could have it . . .

a little over a decade after your death
you watch yourself being honored through poetry
by a globally conscious writer-community

and . . .

as, once again, imagination would and could have it . . .

you thus bear witness to the fact
that you have done far more than your share

so, in the comfort of this precious insight
you now rest peacefully through eternity

can you imagine?

Green Revolution

land is aplenty

reject the false narrative

Earth can feed us all

Singing Along with Louis Armstrong

I am on a road trip,
passing by acres and acres of land;
unoccupied, yet not at all barren,
waiting to house life for the hungry.
Starving people across the globe are aplenty.

I shut down my mind and wake up my soul.
The tenderly tip-toeing melody
from the exceptional vocal cords
of world's biggest legends of all-time
begins to embrace me ever so warmly.

Louis Armstrong whispers into my ear . . .

The colors of the rainbow
So pretty in the sky
Are also on the faces
Of people going by
I see friends shaking hands
Saying, "How do you do?"
They're really saying
"I love you"

There is no rainbow for me to witness at this moment,
but I have been fortunate enough in the past to see many.
I know how the sky becomes exceptionally pretty
whenever that magical bow,
nature's suspending bridge of colors
dons its mesmerizing beauty.
We are driving too fast
to detect expressions on people's faces;
but when we stop to take a break,

some extend their arms to shake our hands.
They don't hold back the gift of universal unity,
otherwise known as our inborn dignity and integrity.
The color of love beams all around ever so brightly.

I thus join Louis Armstrong in his unforgettable song . . .

The colors of the rainbow
So pretty in the sky
Are also on the faces
Of people going by
I see friends shaking hands
Saying, "How do you do?"
They're really saying
"I love you"

Teresa E. Gallion

Teresa E. Gallion was born in Shreveport, Louisiana and moved to Illinois at the age of 15. She completed her undergraduate training at the University of Illinois Chicago and received her master's degree in Psychology from Bowling Green State University in Ohio. She retired from New Mexico state government in 2012.

She moved to New Mexico in 1987. While writing sporadically for many years, in 1998 she started reading her work in the local Albuquerque poetry community. She has been a featured reader at local coffee houses, bookstores, art galleries, museums, libraries, Outpost Performance Space, the Route 66 Festival in 2001 and the State of Oklahoma's Poetry Festival in Cheyenne, Oklahoma in 2004. She occasionally hosts an open mic.

Teresa's work is published in numerous Journals and anthologies. She has two CDs: *On the Wings of the Wind* and *Poems from Chasing Light*. She has published three books: *Walking Sacred Ground, Contemplation in the High Desert* and *Chasing Light*.

Chasing Light was a finalist in the 2013 New Mexico/Arizona Book Awards.

The surreal high desert landscape and her personal spiritual journey influence the writing of this Albuquerque poet. When she is not writing, she is committed to hiking the enchanted landscapes of New Mexico. You may preview her work at

http://bit.ly/1aIVPNq or *http://bit.ly/13IMLGh*

Green Revolution

Borlaug received the credit for the Green Revolution.
World peace through increasing the food supply
to save lives from starvation merited him
the Nobel Peace Prize.

Crop failure in third world countries led
to food insecurity and starvation.
Borlaug's lifelong dedication to feeding the hungry
earned him the title, father of the Green Revolution.

His work led to disease resistant, high yield crops
through genetic modification
that resulted in worldwide initiatives
to increases agricultural production.

Science and controversy collide in the 21st century.
As the society continues to evolve,
the negative impact of genetically modified
food has come to the table.

Hope Waits

Climb to highest point on hope mountain.
My guide points to a beacon of light
across the deep chasm
that can be seen for many miles.

She whispers in my ear:
If you hold patience close
and faith surrounds your heart,
hope always waits for you to come.

I bend both knees toward the light.
Then lie down to sleep
on the mountaintop next to a boulder.
Wisdom massages my soul.

A warm sunrise gently nudges.
My eyes open to morning.
A smile embraces my face with
joyful anticipation for a new day.

Medical Housekeeping

The cleaning ladies and gents
need someone to lean on too.
The forgotten warriors come from
the rear to support the front line.
Give them a thank you and virtual
hug so they know someone cares.

Sanitation, cleaniness, infection control,
a critical battalion in the corona battle.
Unsung heroes on journey to overcome
and survive the pandemic war.

Spray rooms with chemical cleaners,
disinfect walls, floors and all equipment.
Strip everything from each room,
vital to saving lives including theirs.
Pray with the dying when requests
come from a patient all alone.
Working hard for the sick and scared.

Ashok K. Bhargava

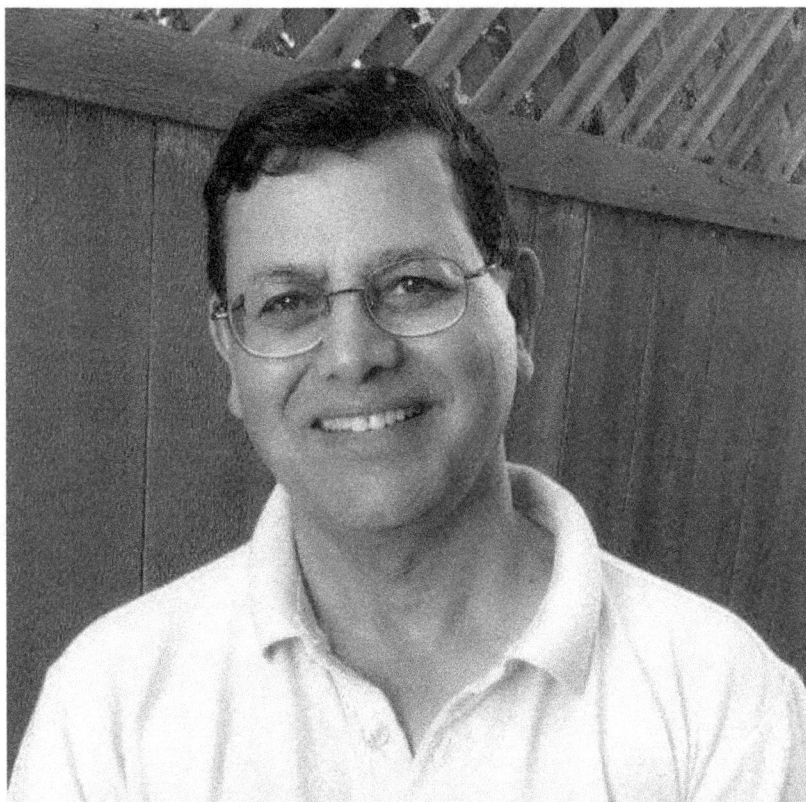

Ashok Bhargava is a poet, writer, community activist, public speaker, management consultant and a keen photographer. Based in Vancouver, he has published several collections of his poems: Riding the Tide, Mirror of Dreams, A Kernel of Truth, Skipping Stones, Half Open Door and Lost in the Morning Calm. His poetry has been published in various literary magazines and anthologies.

Ashok is a Poet Laureate and poet ambassador to Japan, Korea and India. He is founder of WIN: Writers International Network Canada. Its main objective is to inspire, encourage, promote and recognize writers of diverse genres, artists and community leaders. He has received many accolades including Nehru Humanitarian Award for his leadership of Writers International Network Canada, Poets without Borders Peace Award for his journeys across the globe to celebrate peace and to create alliances with poets, and Kalidasa Award for creative writings.

Tears for Peace

Just past the entrance sill
where the footpath leads
to the open courtyard
a man sweeps the dust of others
who walked there
and some of his own.

Under his broom
on the marble tile is a bullet mark
in the shape of a tear –
a legacy of Operation Blue Star
blood has dried up since.
no other unusual sign

except a dry leaf circling around in the wind
whispering defiance
a cry of the muzzled spirit.
I kiss the bullet mark
down to its tongue
to let the pain run through my lips.

I bow my head and fold my hands in prayer
in the bone-chilling wind
blowing on my fingers
once held by the hands of a friend.
This scratch in marble
will never decay

because this bullet shaped tear
is caught forever between
the unwary God and uncaring man.
Sin against God is one thing
but sinning against man
is worse.

We are when We are

Why lose precious time
if there is nothing
meaningful to pursue

Follow the freshness of today
not the fragrance
of wilted flowers

Don't hang loose like
threads drying
crying hard

Create a new destiny
dream a new dream
yesterday won't return

Stoke the inner embers
to light
you wish to light

Life has no set meaning
simply live
and that will give it a meaning

For Pastime Only

at dawn
a dim silhouette
translucent
frivolously
catches a fish

his stares
on the other
side of his face
a dazzling horizon
morning light
peeps into his
darkened space

through his
wrinkled hands
he lets fish
slip away
to live another day

Caroline 'Ceri Naz' Nazareno Gabis

Carolin 'Ceri' Nazareno-Gabis

Caroline 'Ceri Naz' Nazareno-Gabis, World Poetry Canada International Director to Philippines is known as a 'poet of peace and friendship', a multi-awarded poet, editor, journalist, speaker, linguist, educator, peace and women's advocate. She believes that learning other's language and culture is a doorway to wisdom.

Among her poetic belts include 7 th Prize Winner in the 19 th and 20 th Italian Award of Literary Festival; Writers International Network-Canada "Amazing Poet 2015", The Frang Bardhi Literary Prize 2014 (Albania), the sair-gazeteci or Poet Journalist Award 2014 (Tuzla, Istanbul, Turkey) and World Poetry Empowered Poet 2013 (Vancouver, Canada). She's a featured member of Association of Women's Rights and Development (AWID), The Poetry Posse, Galaktika Poetike, Asia Pacific Writers and Translators (APWT), Axlepino and Anacbanua.

Her poetry and children's stories have been featured in different anthologies and magazines worldwide.

Links to her works:

panitikan.ph/2018/03/30/caroline-nazareno-gabis
apwriters.org/author/ceri_naz
www.aveviajera.org/nacionesunidasdelasletras/id1181
.html

a small dream of a small world
Dedicated to Norman E. Borlaug
''saved more lives than any other person who has ever lived''

 in the earth's vastness,
a small voice wakes a small dream
 sees the constant wonder of free life
in an overflowing stream
touches and smells the hope
of never fleeting springs,
the meekness of a small heart
shares the beauty of the evergreens
heals hunger and famine
because of LOVE AND PEACE within,
the green revolution rise from believing
a new dawn for all
the newborn small
from a small dream,
that saved all.

The Wings and Halo In My Womb

I can see you

In Me

Metamorphosed life

My little angel, my little one

How I wonder, how that excitement come to infinity

Happiness and gift beyond compare

The Big Bang wings, the Galactic halo

So pure, naked existence

This paint a love, a life's tale

In the womb of bliss

And chronicles of sacrifice.

Orbitals

let's meet at the skyscraper of love

all can pass, all can enter, with equality keys

let's rebuild the Eiffel Tower

where lovelocks will hold us all together

let's ramp our oneness in our own Hollywood dreams,

be hopeful and hold on to the very stars we try to scatter in

our sky,

let's circumnavigate our earth of meekness

and have the sphere of persistence,

let's flow our connected circuits of understanding

as we spread compassion,

we'll sow hearts to become

a greater humanity

Swapna Behera

Swapna Behera is a bilingual contemporary poet, author, translator and editor from Odisha, India. She was a teacher from 1984 to 2015. Her stories, poems and articles are widely published in National and International journals, and ezines, and are translated into different national and International languages. She has penned six books. She is the recipient of the Prestigious International Mother Language UGADI AWARD WINNER 2019. She was conferred upon the Prestigious International Poesis Award of Honor at the 2nd Bharat Award for Literature as Jury in 2015, The Enchanting Muse Award in India World Poetree Festival 2017, World Icon of Peace Award in 2017, and the Pentasi B World Fellow Poet in 2017. She is the recipient of Gold Cross of Wisdom Award, the Prolific Poetess Award, The Life time Achievement Award, The Best Planner Award, The Sahitya Shiromani Award, ATAL BIHARI BAJPAYEE AWARD 2018, Ambassador De Literature Award 2018, Global Literature Guardian Award, International Life Time Achievement Award and the Master of Creative Impulse Award. She has received the Honoured Poet of India from the Seychelles Government accredited Literary Society LLSF. Her one poem A NIGHT IN THE REFUGEE CAMP is translated into 50 languages. She is the Ambassador of Humanity by Hafrikan Prince Art World Africa 2018 and an official member of World Nation's Writers Union, Kazakhstan 2018. Italy, the National President for India by Hispanomundial Union of Writers (UHE), Peru, the administrator of several poetic groups, and the Cultural Ambassador for India and south Asia of Inner Child Press U.S.

miscarriage of musing

just a minute ;
words are marching
pressure cooker whistles
my amma is shouting " uff ! come fast ; a cockroach in the
room"
the red rose nodding in the spring
seduces me with radiant colours
vendors are shouting on the sub lane
in front of the apartment
selling fresh river fish ....
in the bath room
a line of black ants
where is the sound?
who is whispering ?

every where only the silence of a graveyard

someday the lights will step down
the humming birds will announce
frozen heart will break the arid zone

I will put on the scarlet sky as my mangal sutra

yes ,I shall wait for my groom
with lamp in my hand
no more propaganda of a mask
the liberation moment is so precious ..

just a fraction of a second
only a single word in the net
a flash of lightning with a hooting
"catch me if you can"
the restless fish skips through the keyhole of the door

Oh no ! the miscarriage is so painful
for it takes an era
or
may be another turbulent time zone to conceive ...

a miscarriage after all
blood strains ....in the horizon
may be ready for next germination ......

{ amma:- mother
Mangalsutra :- the necklace that the husband ties round the
neck of the wife on the marriage alter   }

Swapna Behera

the lost child

the lost child looks at the sky
the kites ,the balloons ,clouds
the river ,the trees ,the wood, the sugar candy

who has the time for her?
mother in the office
father with the computer
food served on the table
order placed on line

where is the time to cook?
hot rice ,green vegetables
everything is instant
instant coffee, instant expression of love
instant gift ,instant break up

the world is compressed in the key board
she shouts ,screams within
the tall man of the neighbour
squeezed her soul
who behaves as a perfect gentleman
gives instant solution to mummy and papa
they take every suggestion from that monster
but when they leave he enters ....

where is the time to listen ?
her anger, frustration ,depression ,scars on the breasts
she is an artist, a singer of the church coir
leads prayer in the school

where is the time to sing with her?
the baby doll is slowly transforming ...
a leader is dying within ..

where is the time ?
tears are the mirrors
she wants a life ...
she needs a life

she needs you and me ......

the father of green revolution

and he says
"social justice is adequate food for all;
food is the moral right ''
an agro scientist Dr Norman Borlaug
researched on plant pathology ,genetics,
plant breeding ,entomology and soil science
for high yield ,dwarf variety
and disease resistant wheat
a great lover of humanity
Nobel Peace Prize recipient ,
rewarded in India, Hungary and Sweden
a crusader to end world hunger
his life dedicated to solve plant disease,
drought and desolation
created a wheat–rye hybrid known as triticale
advocated biotechnology ,genetically modified crops
integrated various streams of agriculture
wheat was grown three times more
history remembers Norman as humanitarian hero
for he saved a billion lives
from starvation
yes, he is the
father of green revolution

Albert 'Infinite' Carrasco

Albert "Infinite The Poet" Carrasco is an urban poet, mentor and public speaker.

Albert believes his experience of growing up in poverty, dealing with drugs and witnessing murder over and over were lessons learnt, in order to gain knowledge to teach. Albert's harsh reality and honesty is a powerfully packed punch delivered through rhyme. Infinite grew up in the east part of the Bronx and still resides there, so he knows many young men will follow the same dark path he followed looking for change. The life of crime should never be an option to being poor but it is, very often.

Infinite poetry @lulu.com

Alcarrasco2 on YouTube

Infinite the poet on reverbnation

Infinite Poetry

http://www.lulu.com/us/en/shop/al-infinite-carrasco/infinite-poetry/paperback/product-21040240.html

Norman E. Borlaug

Born: March 25, 1914
Died: September 12, 2009.
Mr. Borlaug was born on a farm in Cresco Iowa to Henry and Clara.
His movement was wheat improvement.
After primary and secondary education,
Borlaug enrolled in the university of Minnesota where he studied forestry,
Received his Bachelor of science degree,
Worked for the U.S Forestry service,
Then went back to Minnesota to study plant pathology.
He received his masters and doctorate too in 1942.
His studies helped countless families,
He felt food was a right from birth and that no man woman or child should go hungry.
Borlaug was a humanitarian who was awarded the Nobel Peace Prize,
The Presidential metal of Freedom,
The Vannevar Bush Award,
Public Welfare Medal,
Congressional Gold Medal and the Padma Vibhushan
Mr Borlaug saved about 1 billion people from famine and starvation.

My homie, the old timer

They won't let me see him because of the pandemic. A video call isn't suffice especially since I've known him for almost my entire life. I'm hearing that his final day is near, I want to be by his bedside holding his hand at the point where he see's the light, so I can tell him to walk to it and that I'll see him when I get there, or my touch will be assurance that he's not alone fighting, I'll be holding his hand like... I'm right here. To me death isn't something new, I've lost a lot of men I knew, it doesn't get easier, so I hope he pulls thru because his family and I aren't ready to mourn him too. We lived in the same building, i was on six, he was one floor under, He's about twenty years older, no cross in him, a loyal brother, he was out there with me in this cold world when all year long was summer. If I got locked up he came to court with bail money and my retained lawyer, it didn't matter where I got bagged, in 161st he used the bruckner, the tombs he used the west side and FDR, if I was OT he'll be on the interstate with black smoke coming out the exhaust of "Betsy" to get me. He never switched, he was there when things were good and when life was a bitch. Im praying for him, what's breaking him down, only GOD can fix.

I bleed urban poetry

When it comes to urban poetry I'm the hardest, I'm not just talking about status, I'm talking about the impact of my words when they're read or heard thru recording and amplifying apparatuses. I've been in the game a long time reppn my genre... blood money, poverty, drugs, guns, jail and murder. I give y'all the sunshine, pain and everything in between those final three days of rain. I give y'all the highs and lows, like the different tones of screams heard when funeral directors at last viewings say... in a few minutes the casket will close. The bottom was ugly, we dreamt of beauty. Dreams became true. the top was lovely until bulbs became the only light some will see or until high beams followed the caddy as it drove around home base slowly with a playas body, that's when the top got ugly. The phrase the more money, the more problems is an understatement to me. Money came in but Im losing sandbox kin, with all the life loss, sitting on a million isn't a win. It's crazy when I think back to when the game begun and how we thought that if we reached a million... no matter what, we won.

Eliza Segiet

Eliza Segiet - A graduate of Jagiellonian University, The author of poetry volumes. *Romans z sobą* [*Romance with Oneself*] (2013), *Myślne miraże* [*Mental Mirages*](2014), *Chmurność* [*Cloudiness*] (2016), *Magnetyczni* (2018) *Magnetic People-* translation published in The USA in 2018, *Nieparzyści* [*Unpaired*] (2019), A monodrama *Prześwity* [*Clearance*] (2015), a farce *Tandem* [*Tandem*] (2017), Mini novel *Bezgłośni* [*Voiceless*](2019). Her poems can be found in numerous anthologies both in Poland and abroad. She is a member of The Association of Polish Writers and The World Nations Writers Union. The laureate of The International Annual Publication of 2017 for the poem Questions, and for the Sea of Mist in Spillwords Press in 2018. For her volume of Magnetic People she won a literary award of a Golden Rose named after Jaroslaw Zielinski (Poland 2019 r.). Her poem The *Sea of Mists* was chosen as one of the best amidst the hundred best poems of 2018 by International Poetry Press Publication Canada. In The 2019 Poet's Yearbook, as the author of *Sea of Mists*, she was awarded with the prestigious Elite Writer's Status Award as one of the best poets of 2019 (July 2019).

She was awarded *World Poetic Star Award* by World Nations Writers Union – the world's largest Writers' Union from Kazakhstan (August 2019).
In September 2019 she was 1st Place Laureate (Foreign Poetry category) – in Contest *Quando È la Vita ad Invitare* for poem *Be Yourself* (Italy).
Her poem *Order* from volume *Unpaired* was selected as one of the 100 best poems of 2019 in International Poetry Press Publications (Canada).
In November 2019 she is a nominee for Pushcart Prize.

Justice

*In memory of Norman E. Borlaug - Nobel Peace Prize
laureate in 1970.*

He saw
the world divided,
people divided,

those who do not know
the meaning of *poverty*,
and those,
to whom
exorbitance is merely a word

– The constant threat of a hungry tomorrow.

Appeasement of the hungry
was his goal.
He still aimed for a human
to win the war against the enemy,
that devoured more than just human lives.

He knew,
that peace could only happen,
when there would be justice.

An empty stomach of full nations
doesn't give orderliness a chance.

The right of all humans
is the food.

Translated by Ula de B

Copiously

Copiously hungry
I await even for an apple core.
Maybe I will tempt someone
and eventually
they will throw me out of this paradise
of death?

I do not want to waste time,
I do not want to be in a place
about which
nothing good can be said.

Copiously hungry
I wait to make the world aware
that people
simply want
– to live.

Translated by Artur Komoter

Flaw

To talk about a world
where people,
more important than things,
can enjoy themselves.

A space
of mutual tolerance –
different cultures,
love without division
of color, faith.

A strange message!

Often
a human does not understand a human,
except for one
– themselves with their needs.

It has a flaw
in distinguishing values.

Translated by Artur Komoter

William S. Peters Sr.

Bill's writing career spans a period of over 50 years. Being first Published in 1972, Bill has since went on to Author in excess of 50 additional Volumes of Poetry, Short Stories, etc., expressing his thoughts on matters of the Heart, Spirit, Consciousness and Humanity. His primary focus is that of Love, Peace and Understanding!

Bill says . . .

I have always likened Life to that of a Garden. So, for me, Life is simply about the Seeds we Sow and Nourish. All things we "Think and Do", will "Be" Cause and eventually manifest itself to being an "Effect" within our own personal "Existences" and "Experiences" . . . whether it be Fruit, Flowers, Weeds or Barren Landscapes! Bill highly regards the Fruits of his Labor and wishes that everyone would thus go on to plant "Lovely" Seeds on "Good Ground" in their own Gardens of Life!

to connect with Bill, he is all things Inner Child

www.iaminnerchild.com

Personal Web Site

www.iamjustbill.com

Norman E. Borlaug

*Give a man a seed, teach him how to plant, how to nurture,
and he shall feed himself and his family . . . teach him how
to teach, and the world shall be fed.* ~ wsp

The revolution was green
And I saw the possibilities
Growing in the fields
Abundantly
Filling the storehouses
And the tables of families
Around the world

I said to my self
We can do more,
We can increase our yield,
Our bounty,
So, I searched,
And searched
And I found a way

In the arid lands
With temperate unyielding soils
There lived a possibility
That spoke . . .
'We could do more',
So we did,
And now there is bounty
That all can eat . . .

But sadly so,
There along came . .

Politics,
And again
Unnecessarily
The people suffered

Now the question is yours to answer . . .
'what are we going to do about it?'

Sow your seeds

From The Christed One ...

And he told them many things in parables, saying: "Listen! A sower went out to sow. And as he sowed, some seeds fell on the path, and the birds came and ate them up. Other seeds fell on rocky ground, where they did not have much soil, and they sprang up quickly, since they had no depth of soil. But when the sun rose, they were scorched; and since they had no root, they withered away. Other seeds fell among thorns, and the thorns grew up and choked them. Other seeds fell on good soil and brought forth grain, some a hundredfold, some sixty, some thirty. Let anyone with ears listen!" Then the disciples came and asked him, "Why do you speak to them in parables?" He answered, "To you it has been given to know the secrets of the kingdom of heaven, but to them it has not been given. For to those who have, more will be given, and they will have an abundance; but from those who have nothing, even what they have will be taken away. The reason I speak to them in parables is that 'seeing they do not perceive, and hearing they do not listen, nor do they understand.

~ * ~

The Poem

400 years and more
Sowing seeds of anguish,
Seeds of despair,
Seeds of hope,
Waiting for the Sun to rise

My eyes,
Our eyes affixed
Upon the horizon
With great expectations
Of and for
The 'Day'
That soon comes

Yes, we have sown our seeds
Upon the paths of
Righteousness,
Tolerance,
Forgiveness,
Patience...
We have sown them
In the fields of
A wanting soul,
But those who had none
Heard us not

There has been many a roadside,
City streets,
Jail Cells,
And ...
Poplar Trees,
And all other

Instruments of a
Worldly death
Where our seeds
Of the future
Have met their untimely demise

Fathers,
Mothers,
Sisters
And Brothers ...
Children if the One
Called home too early
Because their purpose
Was to be the chosen martyrs
Of a people

The others had a hate
Of self
That overwhelmed
Their spiritual reason
So they heard not,
But pretended they knew

We have,
Yes we have
Taken your bleached-out Jesus
And once again
Made him that of our own ...
Don't you remember
From whence He came?

Oh you foolish one,
You, Child of Perdition,
When will you learn,

That the fires you have started,
Will consume you.
When will you learn,
That the parables spoken
Unto you, I
By the Mystics of old
Are founded in an
Irrefutable truth,
That none can escape ...

There is no priviledge
That can provide you with
Leniency of sentence,
There is only
The Hell of your own making
Waiting for you

My advice, you better hurry
And get to sowing
Some good seed
On some good ground ...
And put your heart into it!!!!

Your eternal life,
Or death
Will be your reward.

'you reap what you sow'

Touch

The touch
Crossing invisible barriers
Felt only by the heart
Intimately known
Only by Soul

Not to be seen
Through the lens
Of your worldly ways

I have been here before
A garden where
Fragrant petals
Litter the pathways
Of my travels,
A trail Mystics
Have walked before,
And before again

I have tasted the wine
Bore from the fruit
That I picked
From the makings
Of the sweat of my brow

The world has forgotten me,
But I have not yielded
My sovereignty
To that of the false light
Of dark deceits

The fears are rampant
And has clothed the minds of many
In its ignorance,
But I remember the 'True Light',

That which abides
In me,
In you

Let me touch you my beloved,
Let me be that candle
In the room
That assists you
In seeing your way
Back to you,
Your authentic self

Together we shall vanquish the Demons
For we know their names . . .
As it is said,
"That which you can name,
You tame"

As the cycle goes
Round and round,
We shall step off
And observe
The 'Zero Point'
From which all
Was manifested,
And we shall
Re-hull that sacred seed,
And lock it away
In the spiritual chambers
For a time . . .
And time
In all of its illusory glory
Shall come again,
And again,
Testing our mettle
As it has always done

We shall tear down
That we may build up,
Using that 'Stone of Certainty'
Of the foundation of One,
The foundation of One,
The foundation of ALL things

The children shall no longer dance
In meaningless circles
As does their mentors
Of the empirical workings . . .
Rote, rite and religion
Shall be cast into the great abyss
Where the vanity of nothingness
Is revealed
For what it is

Smiles shall be authentic,
Borne of the true heart
Of love,
For that which is not
Shall wither
And waste away,
And be forgotten

Let us touch and agree,
For time soon approaches
To test the hearts of men
And angels alike

Come on in,
Where there is safety and solace.
It soon grows tempestuous
In the world
And the faint ones
Shall not survive

July
2020
Featured Poets

~ * ~

Mykola Martyniuk

Orbindu Ganga

Roula Pollard

Karn Praktisha

I Fly

because

... said the Dreamer to the world.

I Can

116

Mykola
Martyniuk

Mykola Martyniuk

Mykola Martyniuk was born on March 14, 1971 in the village Zalibivka of Rivne oblast (Ukraine). Since 1986, he lives in Lutsk in the Volyn oblast.

Poet, writer, literary scholar, literary critic and translator. A member of the National Association of Ukrainian Writers (2014) and National Association of Ukrainian Journalists (2000).

Author of a number of poetry, prose, translation and scholarly books (e.g. *Eleventh Command*, 1997, *Mushroom Rain*, 2004, *World beyond the Braille*, 2012, *Under the Walls of the Fortress*, 2012, *Above the Svitjaz' Window*, 2013, *Or...Or...*, 2014 and others, as well as selections in almanacs, anthologies and other professional and literary editions.

He translates from Bulgarian, Polish, Czech, Byelorussian and Russian. His poetry has been translated into Bulgarian, Polish, English, Greek, Byelorussian and Russian.

Розписане модерно
на палітрі дня
вітрами небо
ховала
за Чорний квадрат Малевича
ніч
А над ранок
барви вицвітали
перетворюючи
учорашній шедевр
на сьогоднішню
банальну копію
палімпсест
з і на полотні генія

Де вже їм знати
що найновітніша
найдовершеніша
і найповніша
гармонія
не здатна
врятувати
і вберегти
цей світ
від передчасної
старості

Night
was hiding
the sky painted by winds
in a contemporary style
on the palette of the day
behind the black square of Malevič
And by morning
the colors went pale
transforming
yesterday's masterpiece
into today's
banal copy
palimpsest
with and *on* the canvas of a genius

How can they know
that the newest
most perfect
and most complete
harmony is unable
to save
and protect
this world
from premature
aging

Життя не проза
і не класичний вірш
Життя верлібр
стилізований
під химерні
сакральні
кола на воді
написані
стилом стихії

~ * ~

Life is not a prose
and not a classical verse
Life is a free verse
stylized
into strange
sacral
circles on water
drawn
by the stylo of an element

Моє аутодафе

Не відмовляюся від Світу
хоч він давно
мене вже зрікся
Тепер ми
Квити

~ * ~

My auto-da-fé

I do not forsake the World
Even though he long ago
has forsaken me
Now we are
Even

Mykola Martyniuk

Orbindu Ganga

Orbindu Ganga is a post-graduate in science and the first recipient of Dr. Mitra Augustine gold medal for academic excellence. He worked in financial, banking and publishing domains. Proved his finesse as a Soft Skills Trainer and Content Account Manager (Client Relationship Manager).

Orbindu Ganga is a multilingual poet, author, critic, content writer, sketch artist, researcher, and spiritual healer. His poems have been published in many international publications and anthologies. He has published two research papers in poetry. His painting and article have been published in a spiritual journal - Awakening. He has authored the book "SAUDADE."

Hiding her tears...

Never she had a thought
To get soaked,
She sprinkled
To wet the dust,
Poured to see
The farmers smile,
Drenched many
To cleanse,
A few realised
Her oeuvre,
She was shedding
Her tears
To hide her
Pain,
For years she
Gave the species life,
None bother
To see her tears.

Flowing...

Sliding along the slides
To give a path for the rest,
Giving the flow the pebbles
To cleanse in the middle,
Dust is steady to rinse
Making her cleanse,
Some jerks open the vault
To let the path decide,
Riots within unfold
The seed to grow,
Without any hesitation
Gave the line
The thirst to flow,
Many fissures
Were created,
Never to be
Silenced in the journey,
Flowing is her will
To flow with joy.

Waiting...

Dried rivers search
For a source,
A drop is a hope
To replenish self,
Meadows are down
With wilted souls,
Gathering the memories
To rekindle the thought,
Droplets are hard
To find in these days,
Strained mind can
Open the pores to sweat,
Yestreen thoughts
Still haunts every night,
The lacuna is waiting
For the showers,
Least does it know
Drops are a seed,
Hoping against the hope
We shall wait for the shower.

Roula Pollard

Roula Pollard

Roula Pollard, Greek poet, writer, playwright, translator, literary promoter, social, peace and environmental activist has published four Poetry collections short stories, essays and literary criticism. "Century of Love" was translated into Telugu by Dr L Sr Prasad. Her poems have been translated into Italian, French, Spanish, Albanian, Urdu, Hindi and Telugu. She has promoted more than 200 poets and artists and participated in international Poetry festivals. She is included in more than 90 international poetry anthologies and besides Humanitarian projects, she co-operates with Hollywood and USA artists, European, Indian, and African academics, poets, artists and environmentalists.

Love Is, On The Open Sea

Do I love you my sea, like a window of hope in the wind
or like my heart on an operation table and, what else?
Like blossoming flower I watch you from distance.
Yes, I love you like an ancient sea
like a sea of love horizon
nutritive love, land
of the sea unseen
sails like sea
on the sky
Not like a derelict sea, not like an orphan.
I love you like you love me, as
healing is performed by light
does people's vision protect you?.
Or are you drowned
like war refugees, orphan
children on transit.
The sea is not an orphan
its parents, you and me
protect her, or try to
try to, we protect you
with love

To Aylan, A Two Year Old Refugee Syrian Boy

How much pain
a name contains
Aylan Curdi
isolated island, isolated continent
by our indifference.
You are
the infinite
like an angel in eternity.
You, a symbol
when a child drowns
the whole world drowns

By your name
one continent
all continents
hear your cries.
Does your pain rise
like air, cries
above the earth
as if refugee children, my child
Never die.
Do not die
my angel!
I hold you, my child, alive.
We are holding you
all poets
caressing
your hand

A War Refugee Mother :
How much should my children remember?

Memory has her own home,
do I live in a non-habitable memory land?
I did have a land of memory of me and my childhood
my parents, the lakes and rivers of our land.
Now, many rivers run out of water or do you truly
want to know? Blood and ruins; ruins of history
from darkness of inconceivable and inexplicable acts.

Where am I now? I am an orphan, orphan child of the
world
carrying in plastic bags lost feelings, emptiness of feelings
carrying and rushing my children, my food, my feet to the
new, new land of hope, in search of memory. My children,
I want you to forget the frozen floors of your tender
childhood. Remember the beach and the palm trees
of this Athenian coast, remember ice cream running
down your knees, remember playing football
barefoot, remember your mum like a flower.
These memories are enough for you.

And when you fall asleep, forget the color of blood.
Try only to remember the rain running down
through the holes of our tent.
Remember the path of hope
dreams like the lane that runs
along the tram tracks
in a blossoming afternoon
full of spring
flowers of hope

Karn
Praktisha

Karn Praktisha

Pratiksha karn resides from India and she has authored book THE LOCKED EPISODE at the age of 19 and co authored 20 anthologies. Her writing creates positive impact on social cause. She has also won the title of WORLD POETIC STAR , MOST INFLUENTIAL WOMAN 2020 and VOICE OF INDIAN LITERATURE.

Little

These little sitches of sore
let them numerate ,
In the way and more
To light your attempts
one by one
These stars reflect
the vigour within you.

These little cracks of way.
Let them skate.
all along your play.
To shelter your will,
At every turns and ridges.
This Sphere restores itself until,
You mount your steps .

Leftover Winter

Glance from window is more appealing
Month of February ,
This month,the winter calms
To withdraw the risk of severe cold
When the darkness unites the morn,
With little mist and spray,
Signing a allot for spring to come.
Speak for this version of sprinkle.
So loud for curing,
The sore human outburst.
To play with bad and good in all,
Within the of circle user and creater.
From the tranquil rest to labour,toil.
This soothing chill wind,
Pierce the lost sinews,
To begin again a fresh trust.

Red

Menace are marked with the colour red.
"The red is wars is a terrifying dread".
You even wrap the serenity with colour red.
"The red in warmth is a pacifying shed".
Skipping and escaping from danger threat,
Or captivating sway of magnetic love net.
How the beautiful scenerio so exist..
Differ so wide but clear same admist.
You fear hard by the colour red.
You gear adorations by the colour red.
Twain role of mysterious breath.
The two facet ,is ethos of person in depth.

Remembering

our fallen soldiers of verse

Janet Perkins Caldwell
February 14, 1959 ~ September 20, 2016

Alan W. Jankowski
16 March 1961 ~ 10 March 2017

Now available

1 April 2020

World Healing World Peace
2020

Poets for Humanity

Inner Child Press
News

Poetry Posse Members

We are so excited to share and announce a few of the current books, as well as the new and upcoming books of some of our Poetry Posse authors.

On the following pages we present to you ...

Jackie Davis Allen

Gail Weston Shazor

hülya n. yılmaz

Nizar Sartawi

Faleeha Hassan

Fahredin Shehu

Caroline 'Ceri' Nazareno

Eliza Segiet

William S. Peters, Sr.

Now Available
www.innerchildpress.com

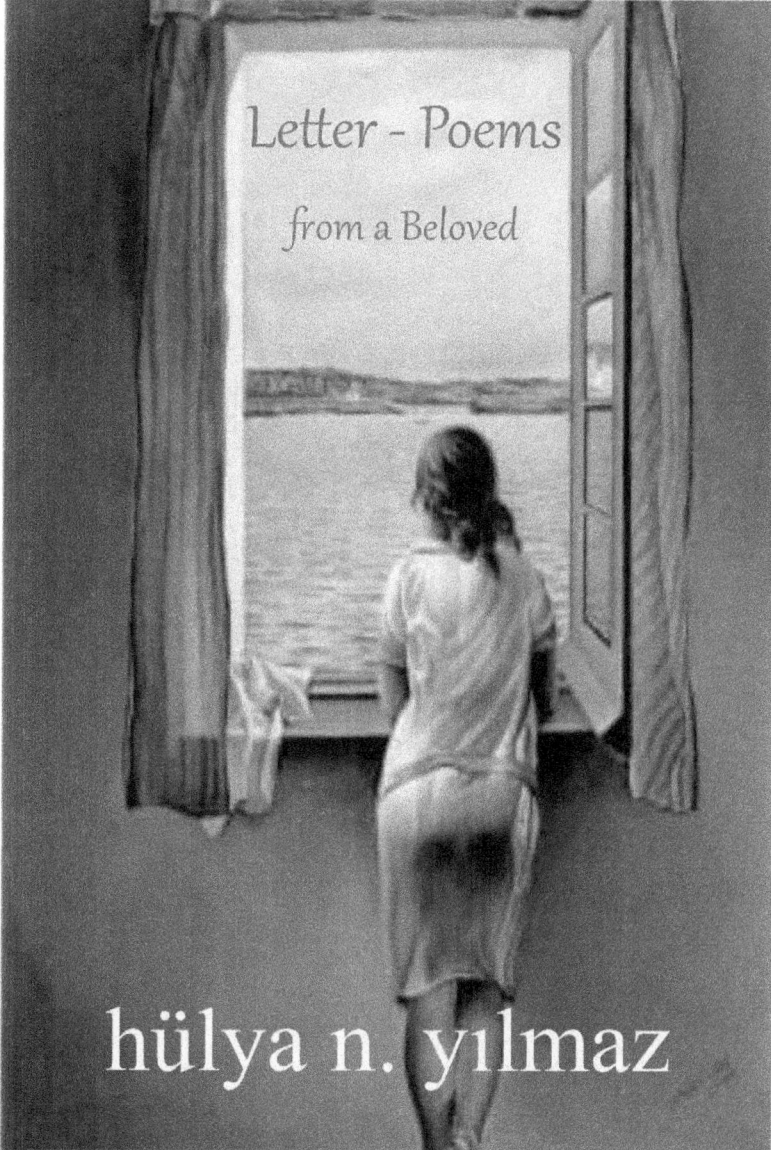

Letter - Poems

from a Beloved

hülya n. yılmaz

Now Available
www.innerchildpress.com

Now Available
www.innerchildpress.com

Inner Child Press News

COMING SOON

www.innerchildpress.com

The Book of krisar

volume v

william s. peters, sr.

Now Available
www.innerchildpress.com

The Book of krisar

Volume I

william s. peters, sr.

The Book of krisar

Volume II

william s. peters, sr.

Now Available

www.innerchildpress.com

The Book of krisar

Volume III

william s. peters, sr.

The Book of krisar

Volume IV

william s. peters, sr.

Now Available

www.innerchildpress.com

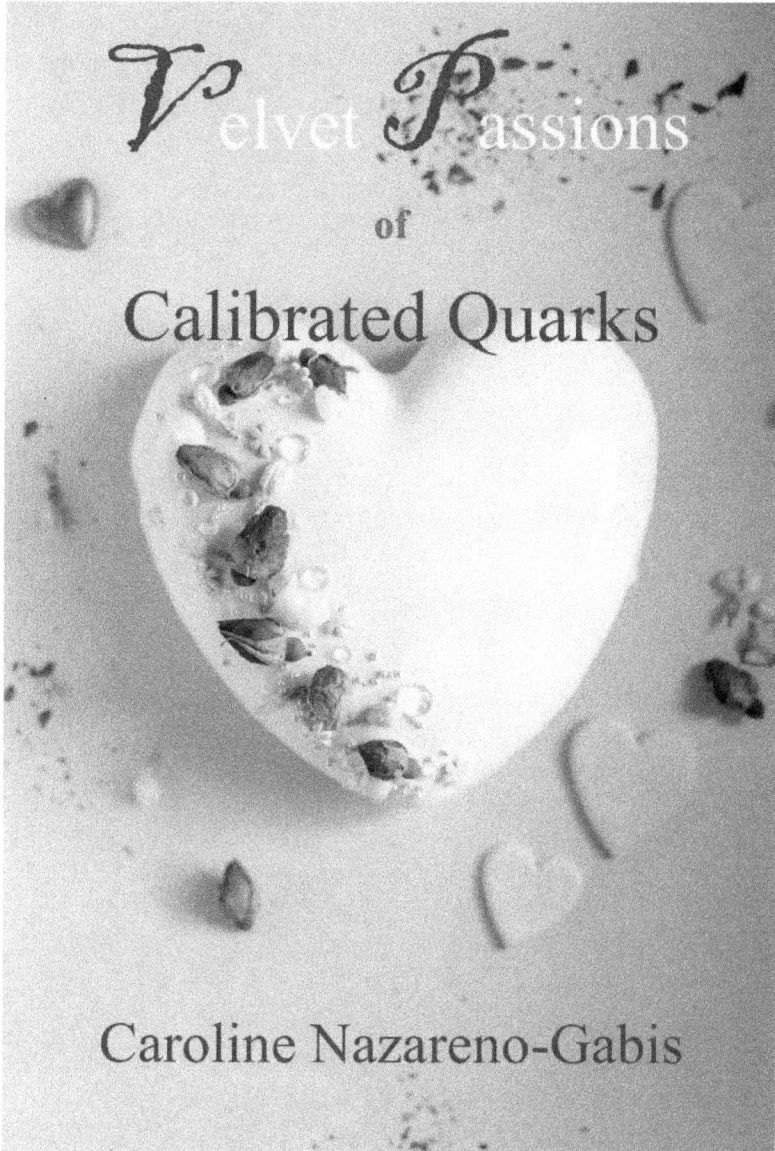

Velvet Passions

of

Calibrated Quarks

Caroline Nazareno-Gabis

Inner Child Press News

Now Available
www.innerchildpress.com

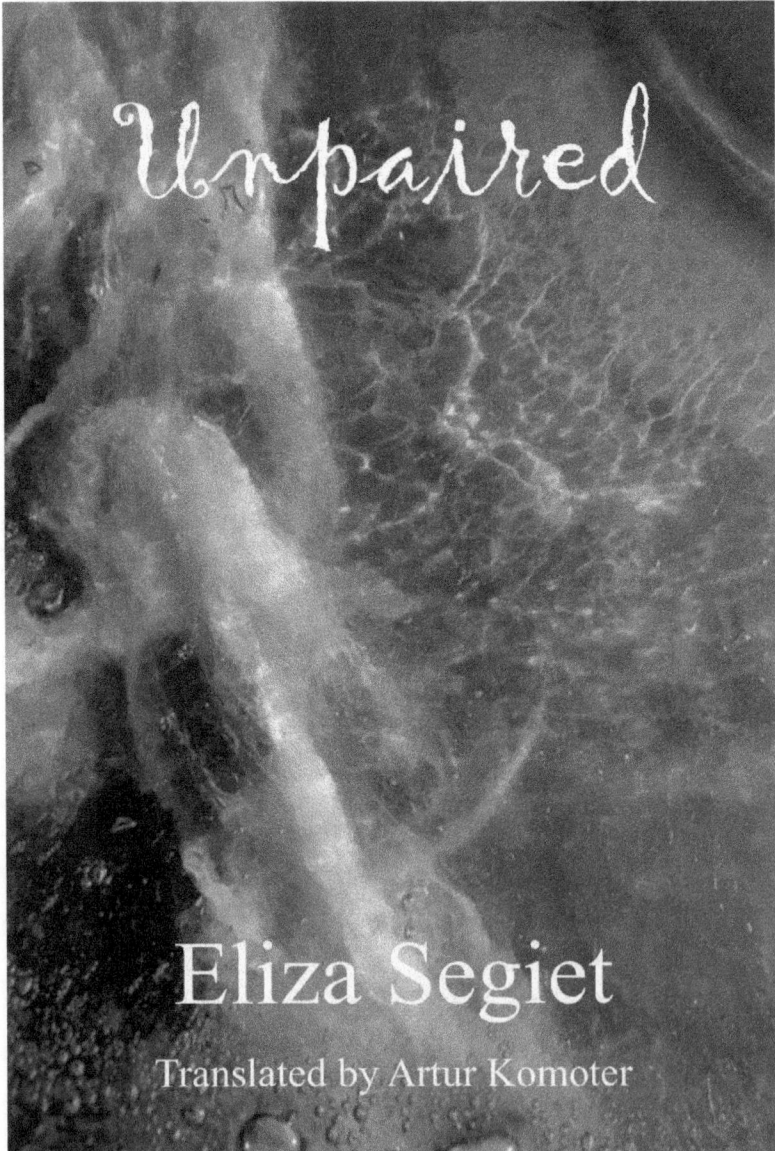

Unpaired

Eliza Segiet

Translated by Artur Komoter

Private Issue

www.innerchildpress.com

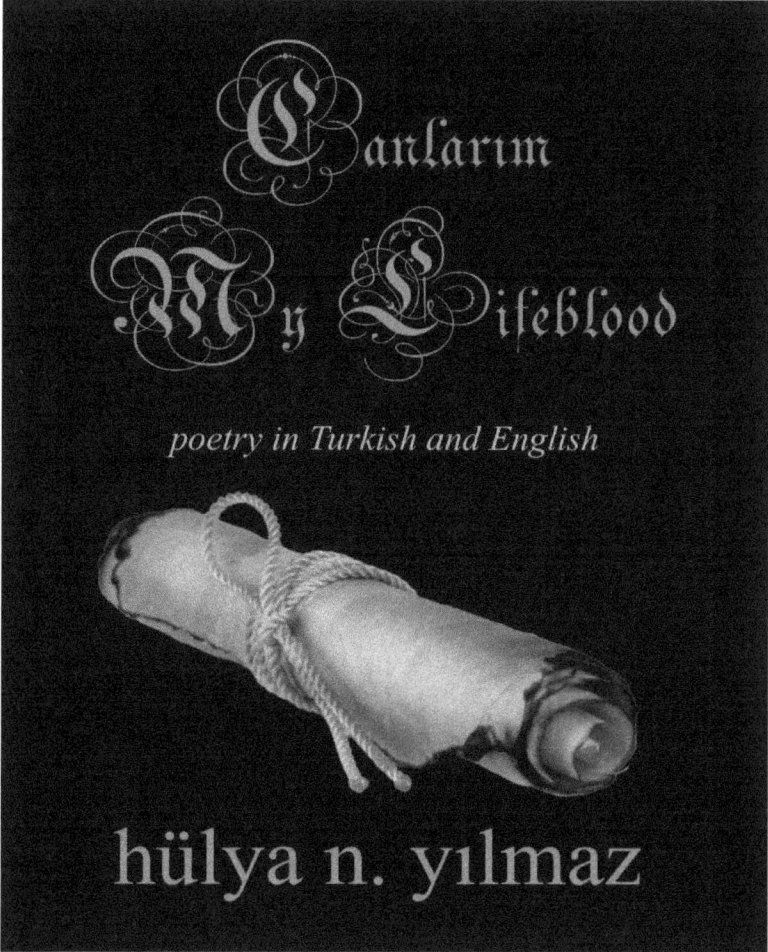

Canlarım

My Lifeblood

poetry in Turkish and English

hülya n. yılmaz

Inner Child Press News

Now Available
www.innerchildpress.com

Butterfly's Voice

Faleeha Hassan

Translated by William M. Hutchins

Now Available at
www.innerchildpress.com

No Illusions

Through the Looking Glass

Jackie Davis Allen

Now Available at
www.innerchildpress.com

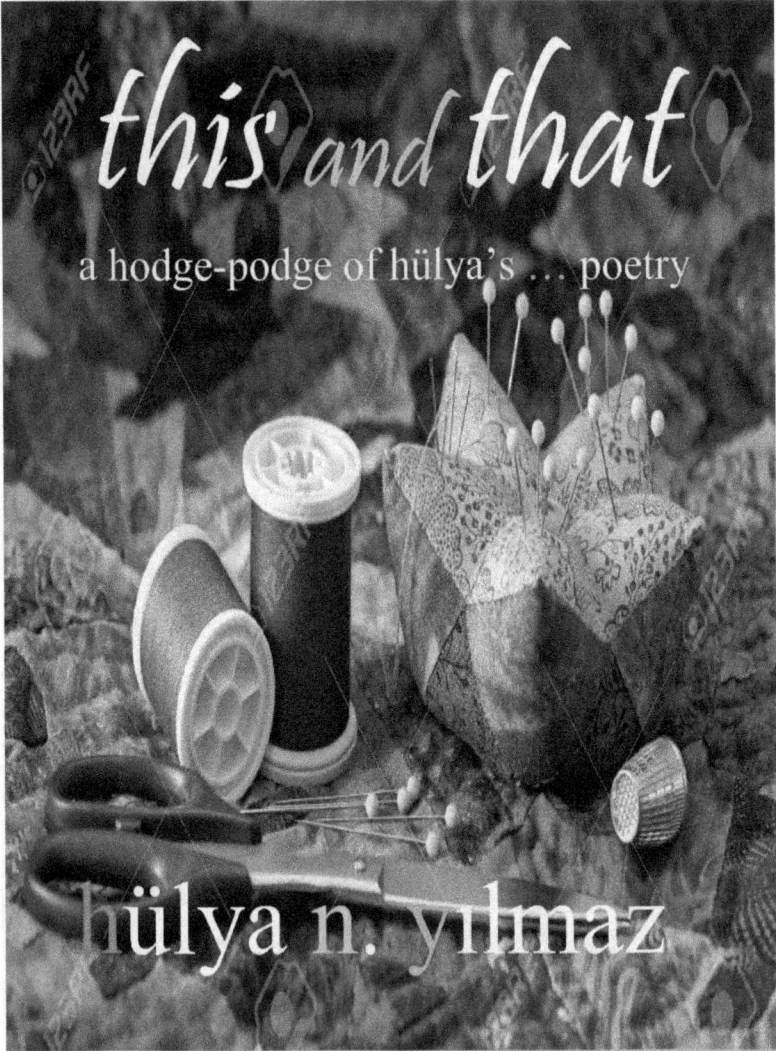

this and that

a hodge-podge of hülya's ... poetry

hülya n. yılmaz

Now Available at
www.innerchildpress.com

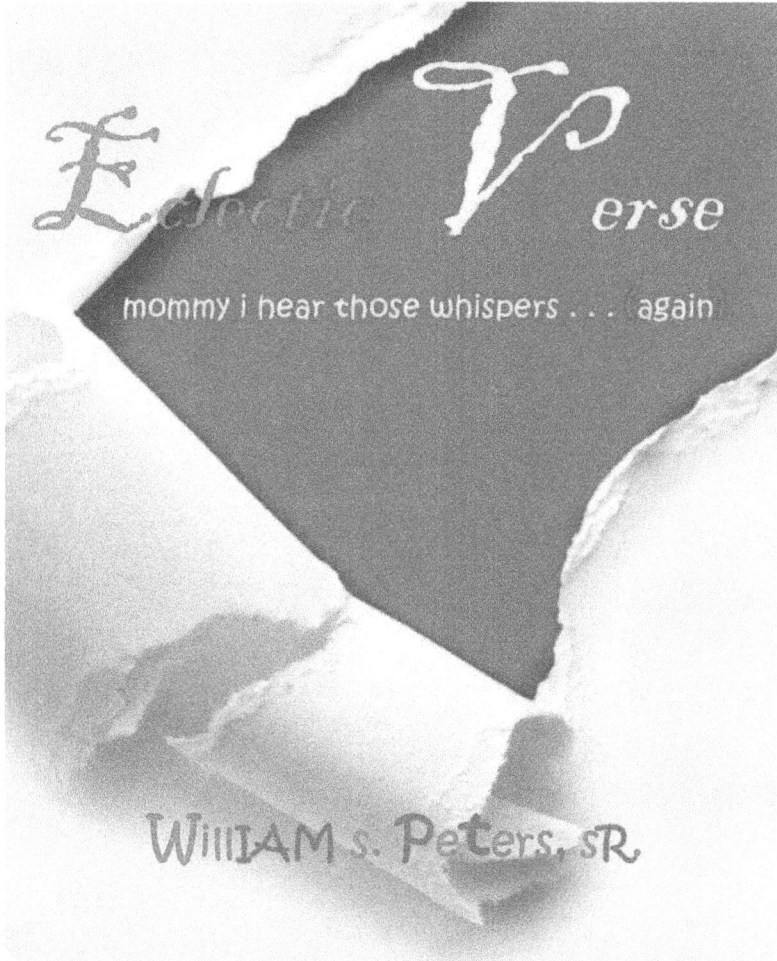

HERENOW

◆

FAHREDIN SHEHU

Now Available at
www.innerchildpress.com

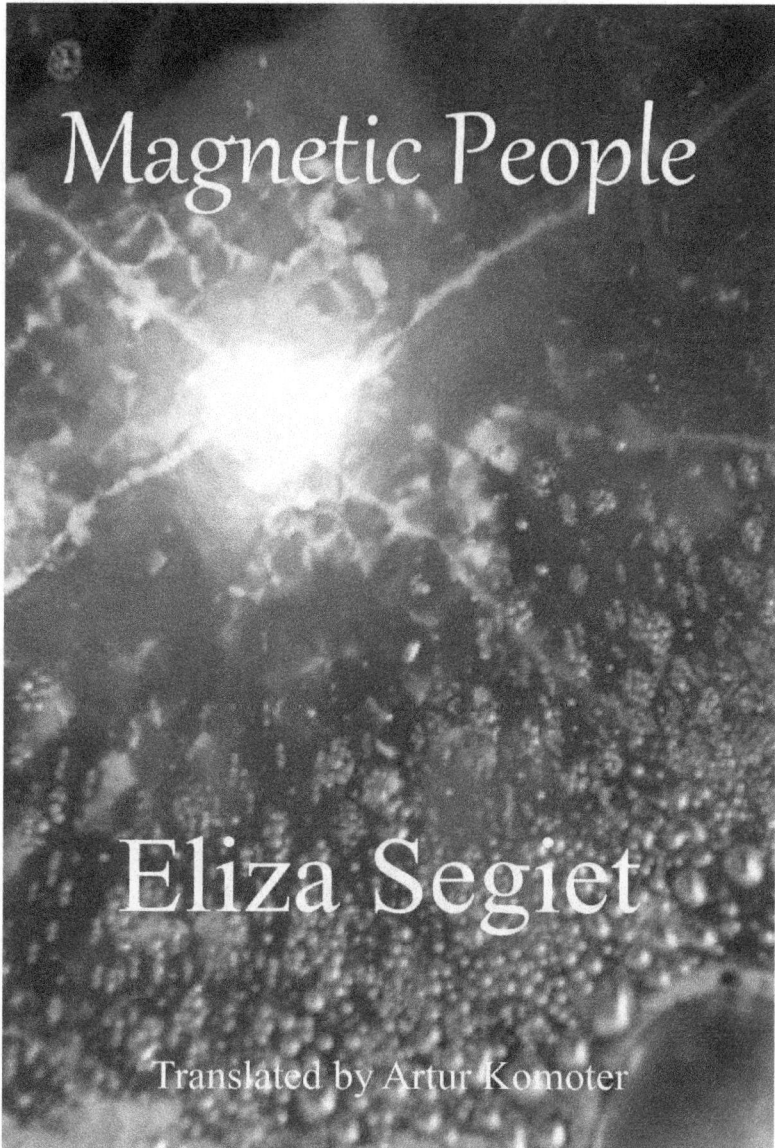

Magnetic People

Eliza Segiet

Translated by Artur Komoter

Inner Child Press News

Now Available at

www.innerchildpress.com

Dark Side

of the

Moon

Jackie Davis Allen

Now Available at
www.innerchildpress.com

Lies My Grandfathers Told Me

Gail Weston Shazor

Now Available at
www.innerchildpress.com

Aflame

Memoirs in Verse

hülya n. yılmaz

Now Available at
www.innerchildpress.com

Mass Graves

Faleeha Hassan

Now Available at
www.innerchildpress.com

Breakfast

for

Butterflies

Faleeha Hassan

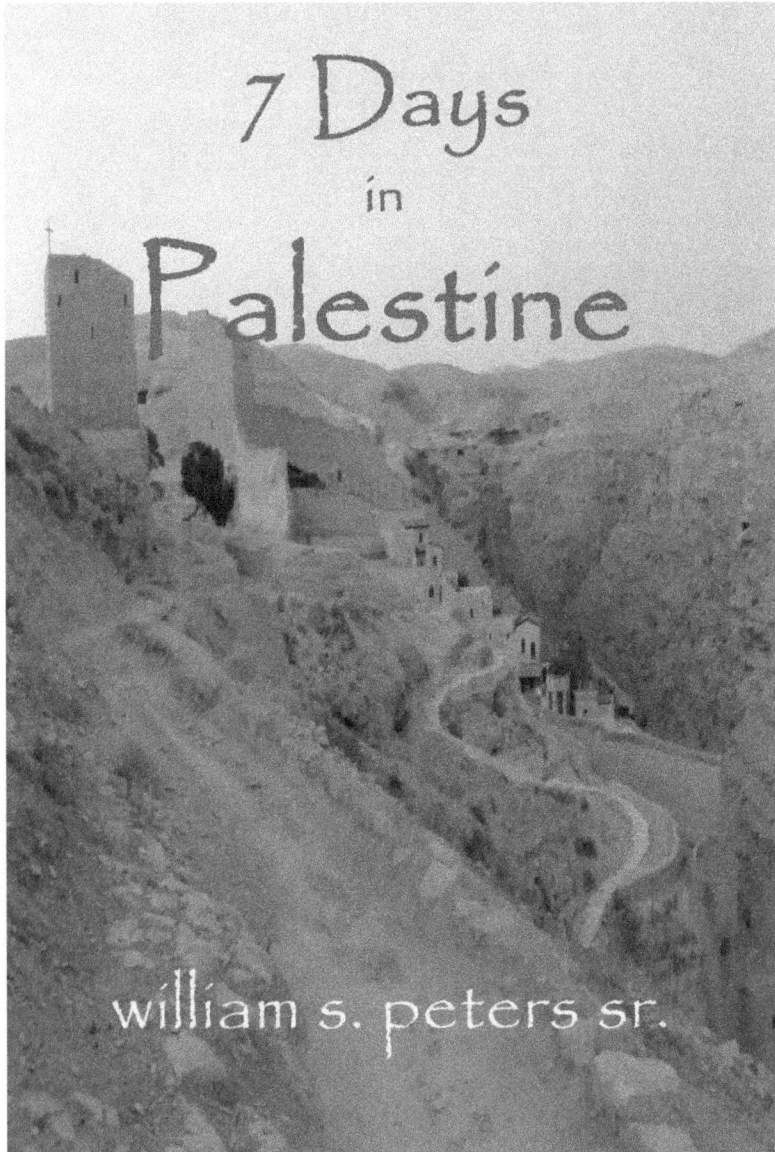

7 Days
in
Palestine

william s. peters sr.

Now Available at
www.innerchildpress.com

inner child press
presents

Tunisia My Love

william s. peters, sr.

Coming in the Summer of 2020

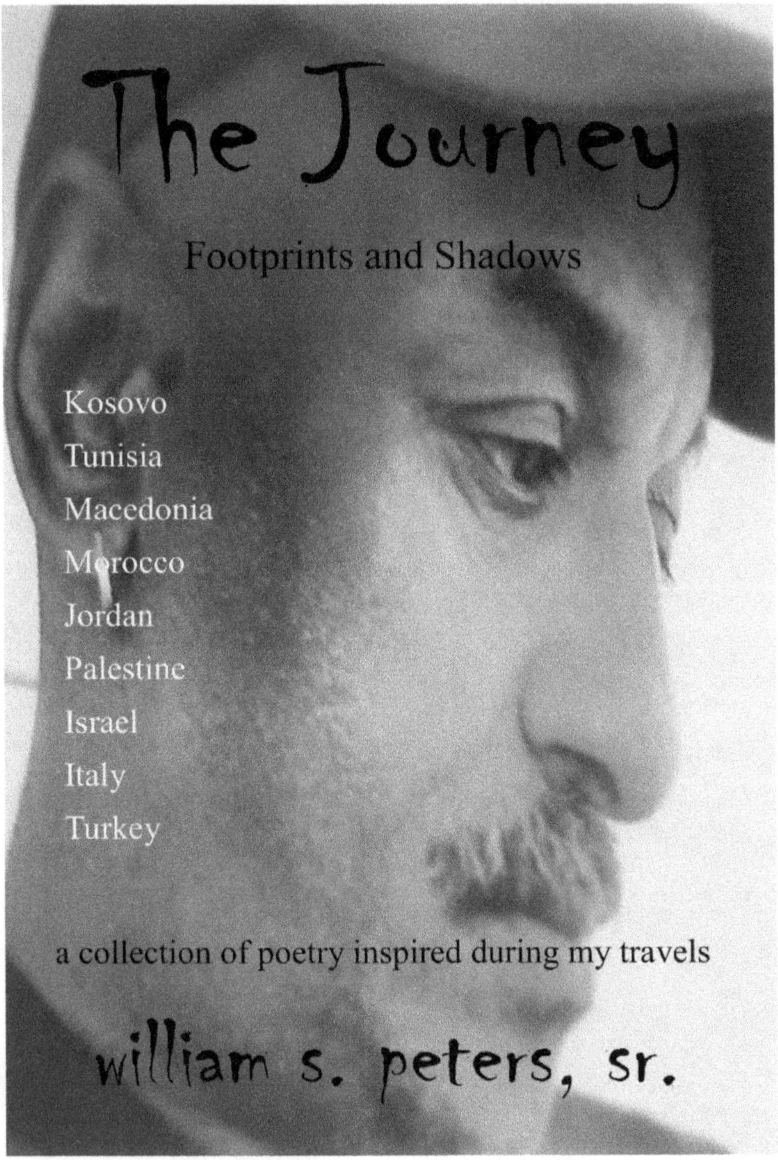

The Journey

Footprints and Shadows

Kosovo
Tunisia
Macedonia
Morocco
Jordan
Palestine
Israel
Italy
Turkey

a collection of poetry inspired during my travels

william s. peters, sr.

Now Available at

www.innerchildpress.com

INNER CHILD PRESS

THIS IS WHY I
SLEEP

william s. peters sr.

Think on These Things
Book II

william s. peters, sr.

Other

Anthological

works from

Inner Child Press International

www.innerchildpress.com

World Healing World Peace
2020

Poets for Humanity

Now Available

Inner Child Press International

presents

W.A.R.

We Are Revolution

Poets for Humanity

COMING SOON
www.innerchildpress.com

the Heart of a Poet

words for a better tomorrow

The Conscious Poets

COMING SOON

www.innerchildpress.com

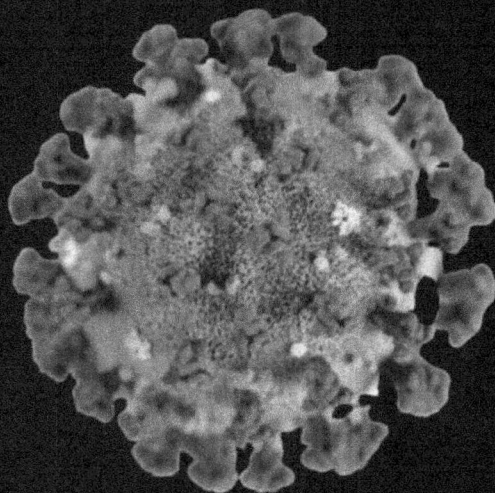

Corona

Social Distancing

Poets for Humanity

Now Available
www.innerchildpress.com

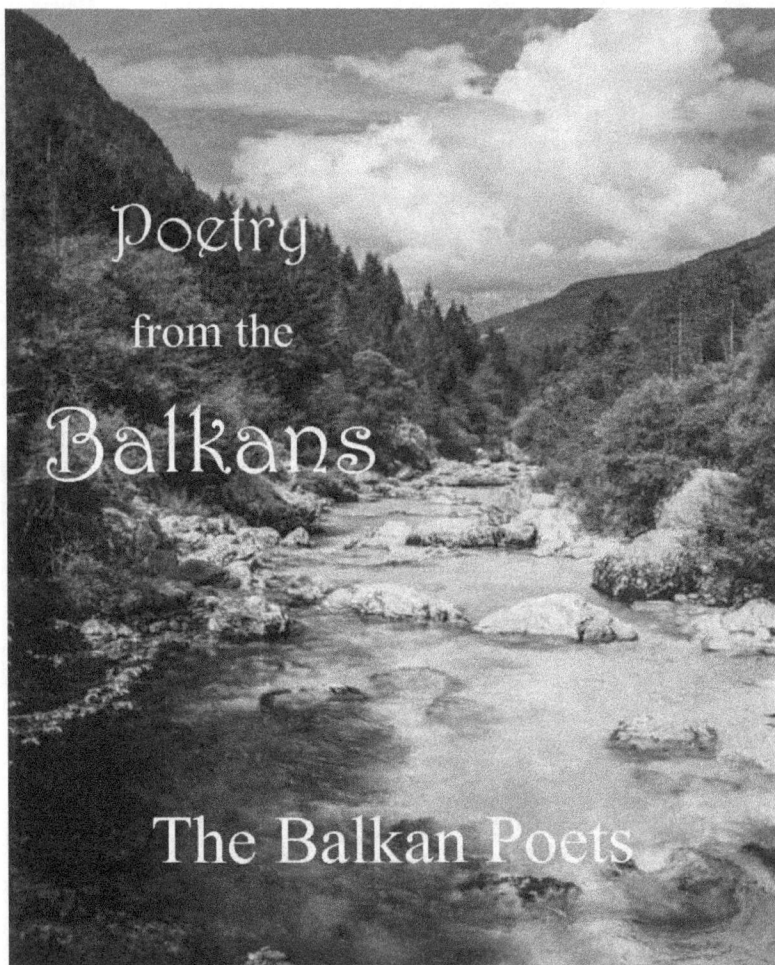

Poetry
from the
Balkans

The Balkan Poets

Now Available at
www.innerchildpress.com

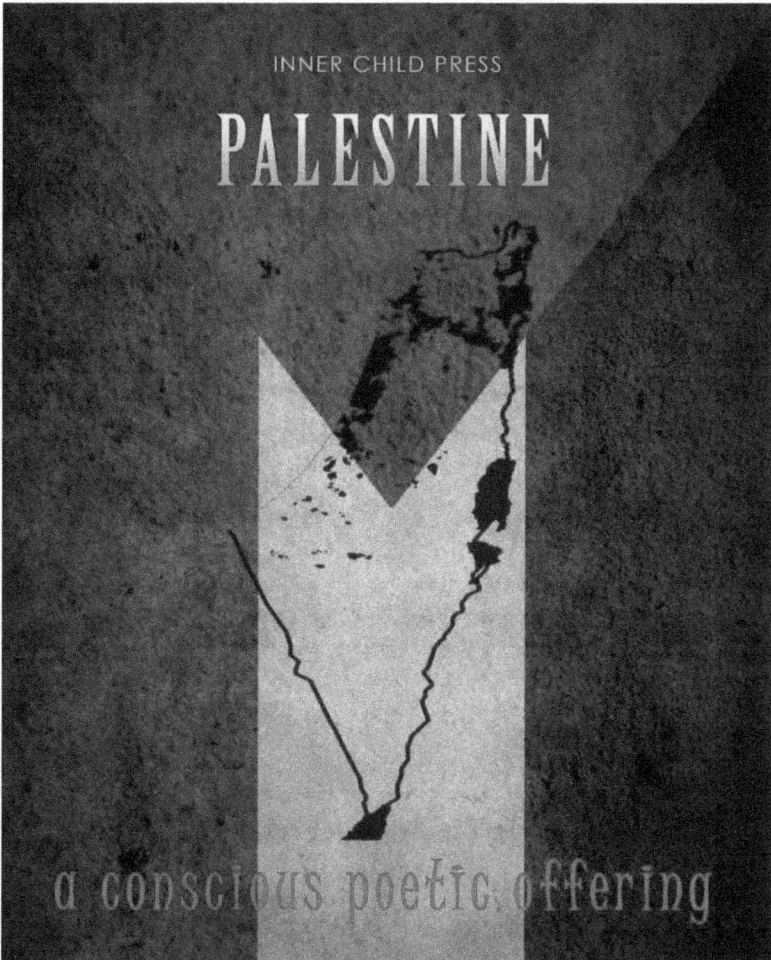

INNER CHILD PRESS

PALESTINE

a conscious poetic offering

Now Available at
www.innerchildpress.com

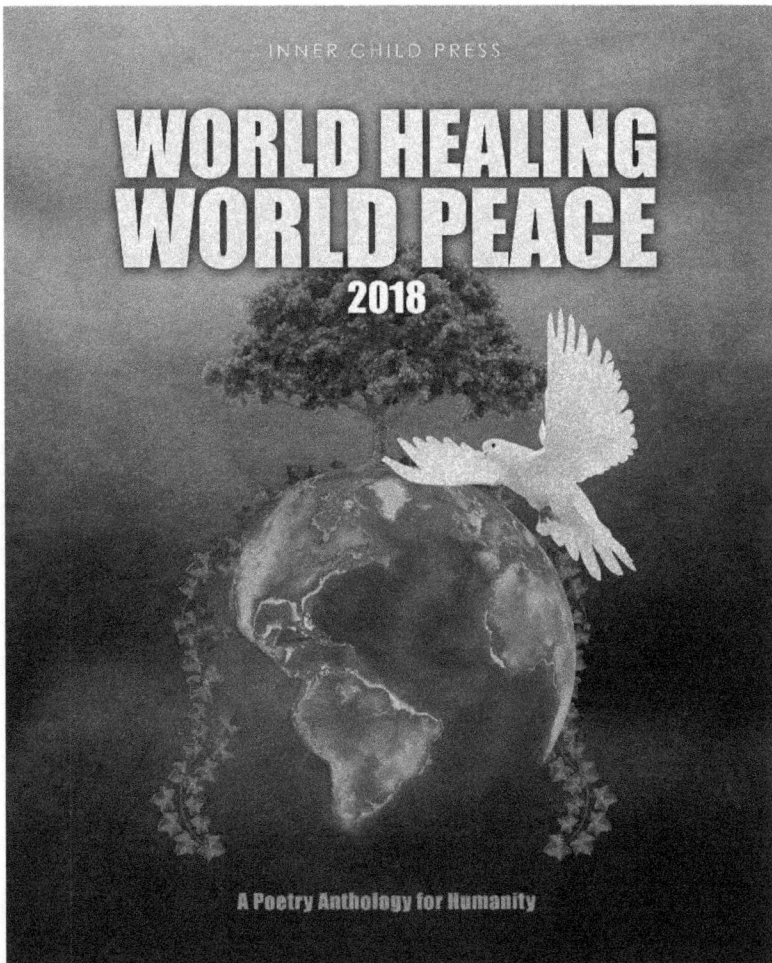

Now Available at
www.innerchildpress.com

Inner Child Press International
presents

A Love Anthology

2019

The Love Poets

Now Available

www.worldhealingworldpeacepoetry.com

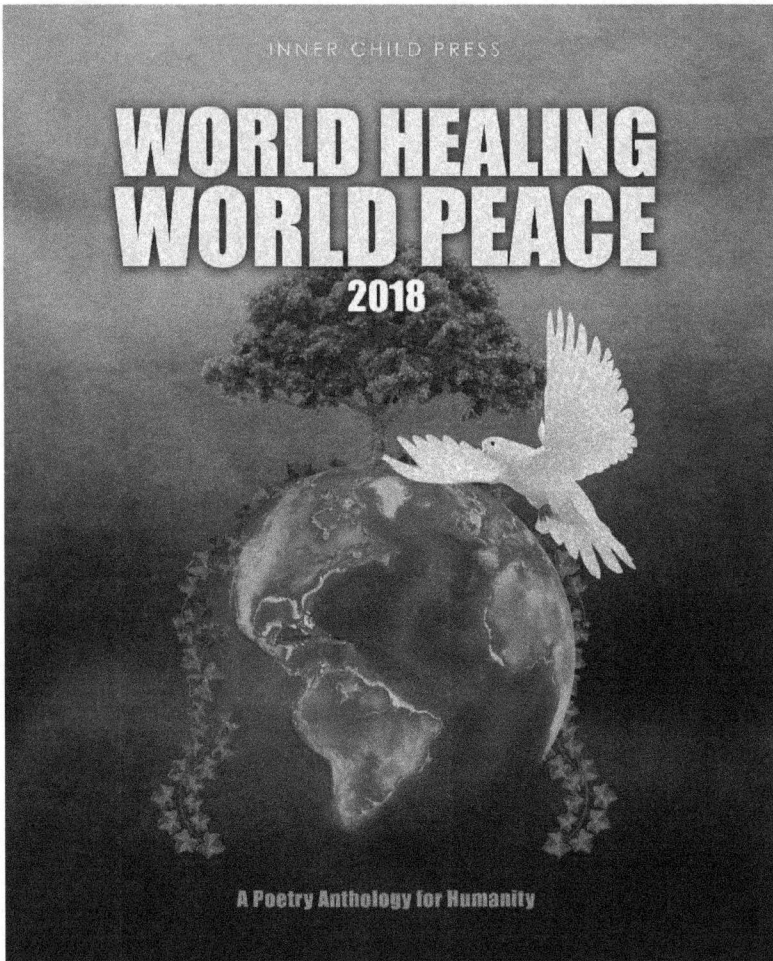

INNER CHILD PRESS

WORLD HEALING
WORLD PEACE
2018

A Poetry Anthology for Humanity

Now Available

www.worldhealingworldpeacepoetry.com

Now Available

www.worldhealingworldpeacepoetry.com

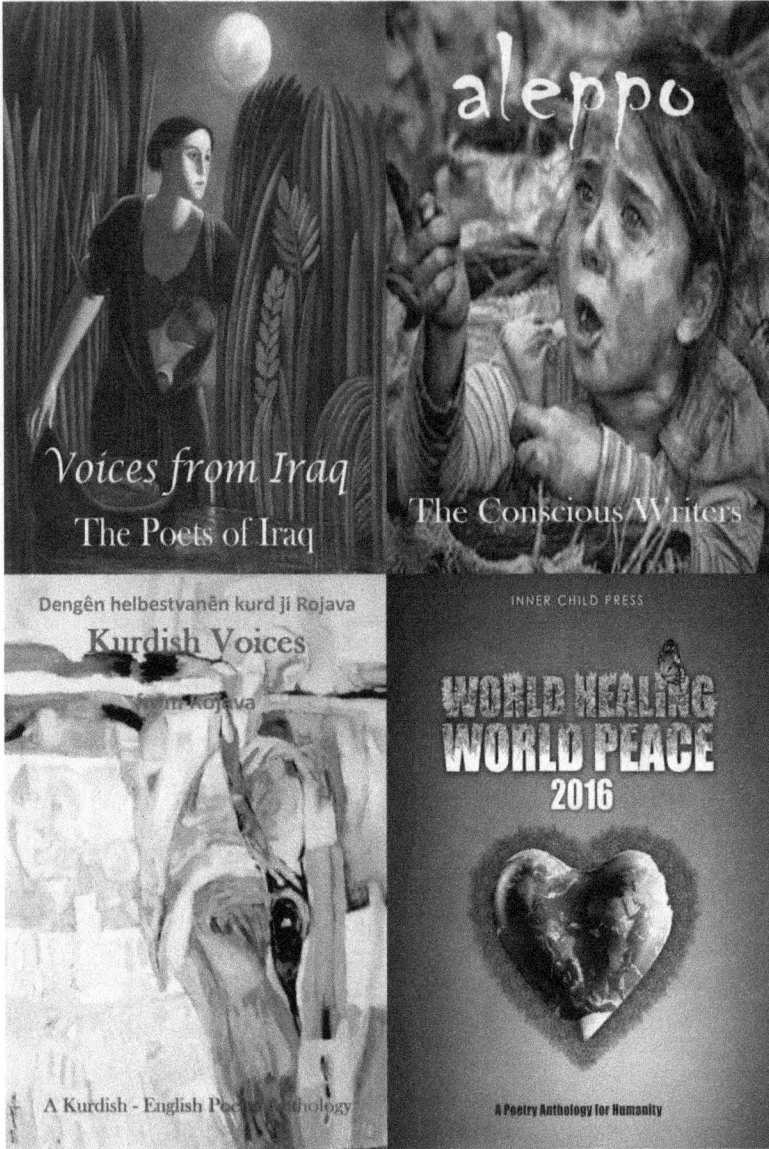

Now Available

www.innerchildpress.com/anthologies

www.innerchildpress.com/anthologies

Now Available

www.innerchildpress.com/anthologies

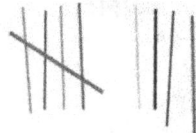

Now Available

www.innerchildpress.com/anthologies

The Year of the Poet
January 2014

The Poetry Posse

Jamie Bond
Gail Weston Shazor
Albert 'Infinite' Carrasco
Siddartha Beth Pierce
Janet P. Caldwell
June 'Bugg' Barefield
Debbie M. Allen
Tony Henninger
Joe DaVerbal Minddancer
Robert Gibbons
Neetu Wali
Shareef Abdur-Rasheed
William S. Peters, Sr.

Carnation

Our January Feature
Terri L. Johnson

the Year of the Poet
February 2014

violets

The Poetry Posse

Jamie Bond
Gail Weston Shazor
Albert 'Infinite' Carrasco
Siddartha Beth Pierce
Janet P. Caldwell
June 'Bugg' Barefield
Debbie M. Allen
Tony Henninger
Joe DaVerbal Minddancer
Robert Gibbons
Neetu Wali
Shareef Abdur-Rasheed
William S. Peters, Sr.

Our February Features
Teresa E. Gallion & Robert Gibson

the Year of the Poet
March 2014

The Poetry Posse

Jamie Bond
Gail Weston Shazor
Albert 'Infinite' Carrasco
Siddartha Beth Pierce
Janet P. Caldwell
June 'Bugg' Barefield
Debbie M. Allen
Tony Henninger
Joe DaVerbal Minddancer
Robert Gibbons
Neetu Wali
Shareef Abdur-Rasheed
Kimberly Burnham
William S. Peters, Sr.

daffodil

Our March Featured Poets
Alicia C. Cooper & hülya yılmaz

the Year of the Poet
April 2014

The Poetry Posse

Jamie Bond
Gail Weston Shazor
Albert 'Infinite' Carrasco
Siddartha Beth Pierce
Janet P. Caldwell
June 'Bugg' Barefield
Debbie M. Allen
Tony Henninger
Joe DaVerbal Minddancer
Robert Gibbons
Neetu Wali
Shareef Abdur-Rasheed
Kimberly Burnham
William S. Peters, Sr.

Our April Featured Poets
Fahredin Shehu
Martina Reisz Newberry
Justin Blackburn
Monte Smith

Sweet Pea

celebrating international poetry month

Now Available

www.innerchildpress.com/the-year-of-the-poet

189

Now Available

www.innerchildpress.com/the-year-of-the-poet

The Year of the Poet
September 2014

Aster   Morning-Glory

Wild Children of September Birthday Flower

September Feature Poets
Florence Malone ⁕ Keith Alan Hamilton

The Poetry Posse
Janie Bond ⁕ Gail Weston Shazor ⁕ Albert 'Infinite' Carrasco ⁕ Siddartha Beth Pierce
Janet P. Caldwell ⁕ June 'Bugg' Bareflield ⁕ Debbie M. Allen ⁕ Tony Henninger
Joe DaVerbal Minddancer ⁕ Robert Gibbons ⁕ Neetu Wali ⁕ Shareef Abdur-Rasheed
Kimberly Burnham ⁕ William S. Peters, Sr.

THE YEAR OF THE POET
October 2014

Red Poppy

The Poetry Posse
Janie Bond ⁕ Gail Weston Shazor ⁕ Siddartha Beth Pierce
Janet P. Caldwell ⁕ June 'Bugg' Bareflield ⁕ Debbie M. Allen ⁕ Tony Henninger
Joe DaVerbal Minddancer ⁕ Robert Gibbons ⁕ Neetu Wali ⁕ Shareef Abdur-Rasheed
Kimberly Burnham ⁕ William S. Peters, Sr.

October Feature Poets
Ceri Naz ⁕ Rajendra Padhi ⁕ Elizabeth Castillo

THE YEAR OF THE POET
November 2014

Chrysanthemum

The Poetry Posse
Janie Bond ⁕ Gail Weston Shazor ⁕ Albert 'Infinite' Carrasco ⁕ Siddartha Beth Pierce
Janet P. Caldwell ⁕ June 'Bugg' Bareflield ⁕ Debbie M. Allen ⁕ Tony Henninger
Joe DaVerbal Minddancer ⁕ Robert Gibbons ⁕ Neetu Wali ⁕ Shareef Abdur-Rasheed
Kimberly Burnham ⁕ William S. Peters, Sr.

November Feature Poets
Jocelyn Mosman ⁕ Jackie Allen ⁕ James Moore ⁕ Neville Hiatt

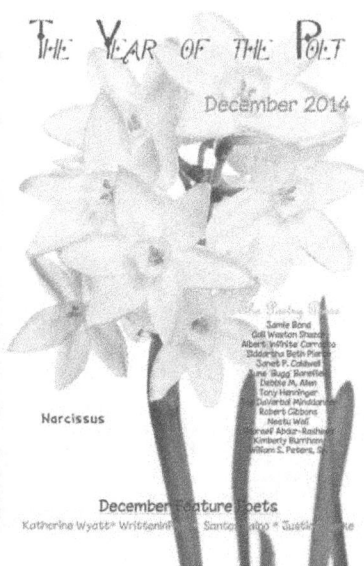

THE YEAR OF THE POET
December 2014

The Poetry Posse
Janie Bond
Gail Weston Shazor
Albert 'Infinite' Carrasco
Siddartha Beth Pierce
Janet P. Caldwell
June 'Bugg' Bareflield
Debbie M. Allen
Tony Henninger
DaVerbal Minddancer
Robert Gibbons
Neetu Wali
Shareef Abdur-Rasheed
Kimberly Burnham
William S. Peters, Sr.

Narcissus

December Feature Poets
Katherina Wyatt⁕ WrittenInk ⁕ Santosh Bishnoi ⁕ Justin Keene

Now Available

www.innerchildpress.com/the-year-of-the-poet

191

The Year of the Poet II — January 2015
Garnet

January Feature Poets
Bismay Mohanti * Jen Walls * Eric Judah

THE YEAR OF THE POET II — February 2015
Amethyst

THE POETRY POSSE

FEBRUARY FEATURE POETS
Iram Fatima * Bob McNeil * Kerstin Centervall

The Year of the Poet II — March 2015
Our Featured Poets
Heung Sook * Anthony Arnold * Alicia Poland

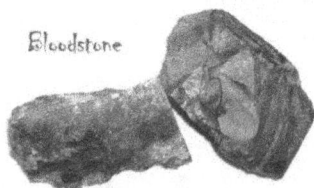

Bloodstone

The Poetry Posse 2015

The Year of the Poet II — April 2015
Celebrating International Poetry Month
Our Featured Poets
Raja Williams * Dennis Ferado * Laure Charazac

Diamonds

The Poetry Posse 2015

Now Available

www.innerchildpress.com/the-year-of-the-poet

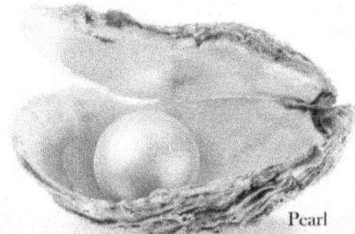

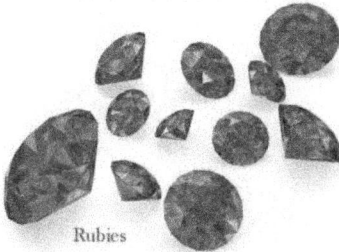

Now Available

Now Available

www.innerchildpress.com/the-year-of-the-poet

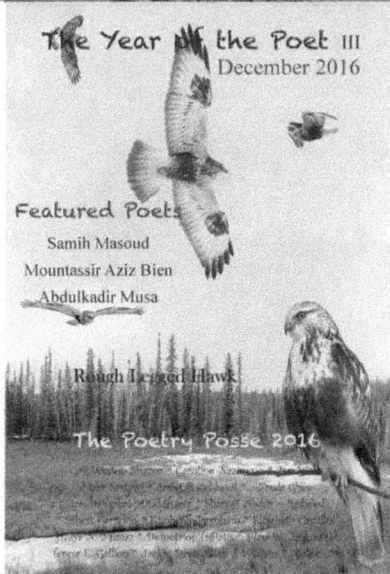

Now Available

www.innerchildpress.com/the-year-of-the-poet

The Year of the Poet IV — January 2017
The Year of the Poet IV — February 2017
The Year of the Poet IV — March 2017
The Year of the Poet IV — April 2017

Now Available

www.innerchildpress.com/the-year-of-the-poet

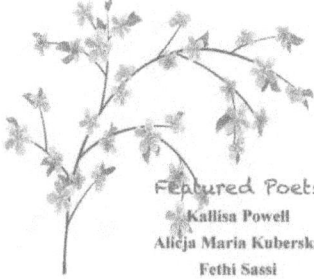

The Year of the Poet IV
May 2017
The Flowering Dogwood Tree

Featured Poets
Kallisa Powell
Alicja Maria Kuberska
Fethi Sassi

The Poetry Posse 2017

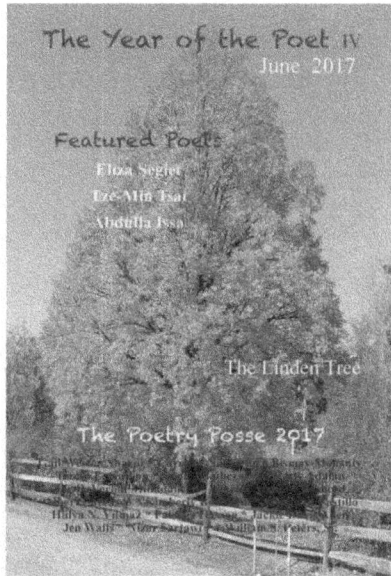

The Year of the Poet IV
June 2017

Featured Poets
Eliza Segiet
Lze-Min Tsai
Abdulla Issa

The Linden Tree

The Poetry Posse 2017

The Year of the Poet IV
July 2017

Featured Poets
Anca Mihaela Bruma
Ibaa Ismail
Zvonko Taneski

The Oak Moon

The Poetry Posse 2017

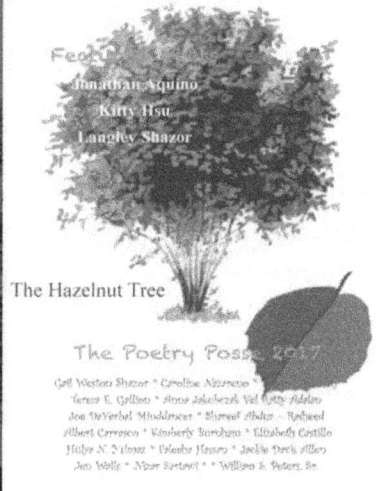

The Year of the Poet IV
August 2017

Featured Poets
Jonathan Aquino
Kitty Hsu
Langley Shazor

The Hazelnut Tree

The Poetry Posse 2017

Now Available

www.innerchildpress.com/the-year-of-the-poet

The Year of the Poet IV
September 2017

Featured Poets

Martina Reisz Newberry
Ameer Nassir
Christine Fulco Neal
Robert Neal

The Elm Tree

The Poetry Posse 2017

Gail Weston Shazor * Caroline Nazareno * Bismay Mohanty
Teresa E. Gallion * Anna Jakubczak Vel Ratty Adalan
Joe DaVerbal Minddancer * Shareef Abdur – Rasheed
Albert Carrasco * Kimberly Burnham * Elizabeth Castillo
Hülya N. Yılmaz * Faleeha Hassan * Jackie Davis Allen
Jen Walls * Nizar Sartawi * * William S. Peters, Sr.

The Year of the Poet IV
October 2017

Featured Poets

Ahmed Abu Saleem
Nedal Al-Qaeim
Sadeddin Shahin

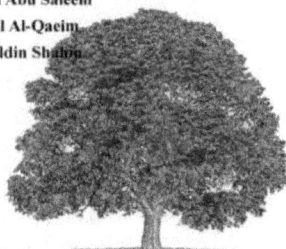

The Black Walnut Tree

The Poetry Posse 2017

Gail Weston Shazor * Caroline Nazareno * Bismay Mohanty
Teresa E. Gallion * Anna Jakubczak Vel Ratty Adalan
Joe DaVerbal Minddancer * Shareef Abdur – Rasheed
Albert Carrasco * Kimberly Burnham * Elizabeth Castillo
Hülya N. Yılmaz * Faleeha Hassan * Jackie Davis Allen
Jen Walls * Nizar Sartawi * * William S. Peters, Sr.

The Year of the Poet IV
November 2017

Featured Poets

Kay Peters
Alfreda D. Ghee
Gabriella Garofalo
Rosemary Cappello

The Tree of Life

The Poetry Posse 2017

Gail Weston Shazor * Caroline Nazareno * Bismay Mohanty
Teresa E. Gallion * Anna Jakubczak Vel Ratty Adalan
Joe DaVerbal Minddancer * Shareef Abdur – Rasheed
Albert Carrasco * Kimberly Burnham * Elizabeth Castillo
Hülya N. Yılmaz * Faleeha Hassan * Jackie Davis Allen
Jen Walls * Nizar Sartawi * William S. Peters, Sr.

The Year of the Poet IV
December 2017

Featured Poets

Justice Clarke
Mariel M. Pabroa
Kiley Brown

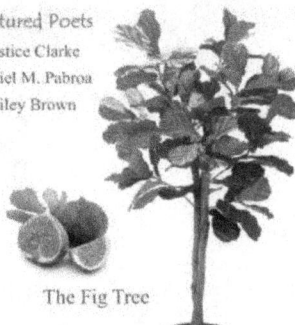

The Fig Tree

The Poetry Posse 2017

Gail Weston Shazor * Caroline Nazareno * Bismay Mohanty
Teresa E. Gallion * Anna Jakubczak Vel Ratty Adalan
Joe DaVerbal Minddancer * Shareef Abdur – Rasheed
Albert Carrasco * Kimberly Burnham * Elizabeth Castillo
Hülya N. Yılmaz * Faleeha Hassan * Jackie Davis Allen
Jen Walls * Nizar Sartawi * William S. Peters, Sr.

Now Available

www.innerchildpress.com/the-year-of-the-poet

The Year of the Poet V
January 2018
Featured Poets

Tyad Shamasnah

Yasmeen Hamzeh

Ali Abdolrezaei

Aksum

The Poetry Posse 2018

Gail Weston Shazor * Caroline Nazareno * Tezmin Ition Tsai
Hülya N. Yılmaz * Faleeha Hassan * Jackie Davis Allen
Teresa E. Gallion * Anna Jakubczak Vel Ratty Adalan
Alicja Maria Kuberska * Shareef Abdur – Rasheed
Kimberly Burnham * Elizabeth Castillo
Nizar Sartawi * William S. Peters, Sr.

The Year of the Poet V
February 2018

Sabean

Featured Poets

Muhammad Azram

Anna Szawracka

Abhilipsa Kuana:

Aanika Acty

The Poetry Posse 2018

Gail Weston Shazor * Caroline Nazareno * Tezmin Ition Tsai
Hülya N. Yılmaz * Faleeha Hassan * Jackie Davis Allen
Teresa E. Gallion * Anna Jakubczak Vel Ratty Adalan
Alicja Maria Kuberska * Shareef Abdur – Rasheed
Kimberly Burnham * Elizabeth Castillo
Nizar Sartawi * William S. Peters, Sr.

The Year of the Poet V
March 2018

Featured Poets

Inam Fatima 'Ashi'
Cassandra Swan
Jaleel Khazaal
Shazia Zaman

Caribbean & Middle America

The Poetry Posse 2018

Gail Weston Shazor * Nizar Sartawi * Hülya N. Yılmaz
Jackie Davis Allen * Caroline 'Ceri' Nazareno
Alicja Maria Kuberska * Teresa E. Gallion
Faleeha Hassan * Shareef Abdur – Rasheed
Kimberly Burnham * Elizabeth Castillo
Tezmin Ition Tsai * William S. Peters, Sr.

The Year of the Poet V
April 2018

Featured Poets

The Nez Perce

The Poetry Posse 2018

Now Available

www.innerchildpress.com/the-year-of-the-poet

The Year of the Poet V
May 2018

Featured Poets
Zaldá Carreon de León &
Sylwia B. Malinowska
Candita Ahmeti
Ojuba Proidan

The Sumerians

The Poetry Posse 2018
Gail Weston Shazor * Nizar Sartawi * Hülya N. Yılmaz
Jackie Davis Allen * Caroline 'Ceri' Nazareno
Alicja Maria Kuberska * Teresa E. Gallion
Kimberly Burnham * Shareef Abdur – Rasheed
Faleeha Hassan * Elizabeth Castillo * Swapna Behera
Tezmin Ition Tsai * William S. Peters, Sr.

The Year of the Poet V
June 2018

Featured Poets
Bilall Maliqi * Darin Millan * Gojko Božović * Sofija Živković

The Paleo Indians

The Poetry Posse 2018

The Year of the Poet V
July 2018

Featured Poets
Patrusja Trencsér-Paddy
Mohammad Iqbal Hasil
Eliza Segiet
Jim Higgins

Oceania

The Poetry Posse 2018
Gail Weston Shazor * Nizar Sartawi * Hülya N. Yılmaz
Jackie Davis Allen * Caroline 'Ceri' Nazareno
Alicja Maria Kuberska * Teresa E. Gallion
Kimberly Burnham * Shareef Abdur – Rasheed
Faleeha Hassan * Elizabeth Castillo * Swapna Behera
Tezmin Ition Tsai * William S. Peters, Sr.

The Year of the Poet V
August 2018

Featured Poets
Hussein Habasch * Mircea Dan Duta * Naida Mujkić * Swagat Das

The Lapita

The Poetry Posse 2018
Gail Weston Shazor * Nizar Sartawi * Hülya N. Yılmaz
Jackie Davis Allen * Caroline 'Ceri' Nazareno
Alicja Maria Kuberska * Teresa E. Gallion
Kimberly Burnham * Shareef Abdur – Rasheed
Ashok K. Bhargava* Elizabeth Castillo * Swapna Behaera
Tezmin Ition Tsai * William S. Peters, Sr.

Now Available

www.innerchildpress.com/the-year-of-the-poet

The Year of the Poet V
September 2018

The Aztecs & Incas

Featured Poets
Kolade Olanrewaju Freedom
Elisa Segiet
Machel Hussain Abdul Ghani
Lily Swarn

The Poetry Posse 2018

Gail Weston Shazor * Nizar Sartawi * Hülya N. Yilmaz
Jackie Davis Allen * Caroline 'Ceri' Nazareno
Alicja Maria Kuberska * Teresa E. Gallion
Kimberly Burnham * Shareef Abdur ~ Rasheed
Ashok K. Bhargava * Elizabeth Castillo * Swapna Behera
Tezmin Ition Tsai * William S. Peters, Sr.

The Year of the Poet V
October 2018

Featured Poets
Alicia Minjarez * Lonneice Weeks-Batley
Lopamudra Mishra * Abdelwahed Souayah

Bengali

The Poetry Posse 2018

Gail Weston Shazor * Nizar Sartawi * Hülya N. Yilmaz
Jackie Davis Allen * Caroline 'Ceri' Nazareno
Alicja Maria Kuberska * Teresa E. Gallion
Kimberly Burnham * Shareef Abdur ~ Rasheed
Ashok K. Bhargava * Elizabeth Castillo * Swapna Behera
Tezmin Ition Tsai * William S. Peters, Sr.

The Year of the Poet V
November 2018

Featured Poets
Michelle Joan Barulich * Monsif Beroual
Krystyna Konecka * Nassira Nezzar

The Poetry Posse 2018

Gail Weston Shazor * Nizar Sartawi * Hülya N. Yilmaz
Jackie Davis Allen * Caroline 'Ceri' Nazareno
Alicja Maria Kuberska * Teresa E. Gallion
Kimberly Burnham * Shareef Abdur ~ Rasheed
Ashok K. Bhargava * Elizabeth Castillo * Swapna Behera
Tezmin Ition Tsai * William S. Peters, Sr.

The Year of the Poet V
December 2018

Featured Poets
Rose Terranova Cirigliano
Joanna Kalinowska
Sokulović Emir
Dr. T. Ashok Chakravarthy

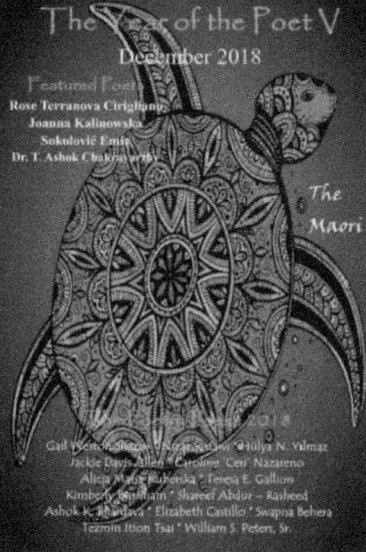

The
Maori

The Poetry Posse 2018

Gail Weston Shazor * Nizar Sartawi * Hülya N. Yilmaz
Jackie Davis Allen * Caroline 'Ceri' Nazareno
Alicja Maria Kuberska * Teresa E. Gallion
Kimberly Burnham * Shareef Abdur ~ Rasheed
Ashok K. Bhargava * Elizabeth Castillo * Swapna Behera
Tezmin Ition Tsai * William S. Peters, Sr.

Now Available

www.innerchildpress.com/the-year-of-the-poet

203

Inner Child Press Anthologies

The Year of the Poet VI
January 2019

Indigenous North Americans

Featured Poets

Houda Elfchtali
Anthony Briscoe
Iram Fatima 'Ashi'
Dr. K. K. Mathew

Dream Catcher

The Poetry Posse 2019

Gail Weston Shazor * Joe Paire * Hülya N. Yılmaz
Jackie Davis Allen * Caroline Cerè Nazareno
Alicja Maria Kuberska * Teresa E. Gallion
Kimberly Burnham * Shareef Abdur – Rasheed
Ashok K. Bhargava * Elizabeth Castillo * Swapna Behera
Tezmin Ition Tsai * William S. Peters, Sr.

The Year of the Poet VI
February 2019

Featured Poets

Marek Łukaszewicz * Bharati Nayak
Aida G. Roque * Jean-Jacques Fournier

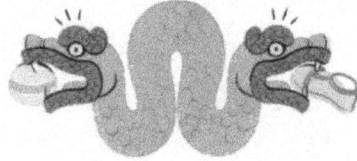

Meso-America

The Poetry Posse 2019

Gail Weston Shazor * Albert Carrasco * Hülya N. Yılmaz
Jackie Davis Allen * Caroline Nazareno * Eliza Segiet
Alicja Maria Kuberska * Teresa E. Gallion * Joe Paire
Kimberly Burnham * Shareef Abdur – Rasheed
Ashok K. Bhargava * Elizabeth Castillo * Swapna Behera
Tezmin Ition Tsai * William S. Peters, Sr.

The Year of the Poet VI
March 2019

Featured Poets

Enesa Mahmić * Sylwia K. Malinowska
Shurouk Hammoud * Anwer Ghani

The Caribbean

The Poetry Posse 2019

Gail Weston Shazor * Albert Carrasco * Hülya N. Yılmaz
Jackie Davis Allen * Caroline Nazareno * Eliza Segiet
Alicja Maria Kuberska * Teresa E. Gallion * Joe Paire
Kimberly Burnham * Shareef Abdur – Rasheed
Ashok K. Bhargava * Elizabeth Castillo * Swapna Behera
Tezmin Ition Tsai * William S. Peters, Sr.

The Year of the Poet VI
April 2019

Featured Poets

DL Davis * Michelle Joan Baruhich
Lulëzim Haziri * Faleeha Hassan

Central & West Africa

The Poetry Posse 2019

Gail Weston Shazor * Albert Carrasco * Hülya N. Yılmaz
Jackie Davis Allen * Caroline Nazareno * Eliza Segiet
Alicja Maria Kuberska * Teresa E. Gallion * Joe Paire
Kimberly Burnham * Shareef Abdur – Rasheed
Ashok K. Bhargava * Elizabeth Castillo * Swapna Behera
Tezmin Ition Tsai * William S. Peters, Sr.

Now Available

www.innerchildpress.com/the-year-of-the-poet

The Year of the Poet VI
May 2019

Featured Poets
Emad Al-Haydary * Hussein Nasser Jabr
Wahab Sheriff * Abdul Razzaq Al Ameeri

Asia Southeast Asia and Maritime Asia

The Poetry Posse 2019

Gail Weston Shazor * Albert Carrasco * Hülya N. Yılmaz
Jackie Davis Allen * Caroline Nazareno * Eliza Segiet
Alicja Maria Kubeska * Teresa E. Gallion * Joe Paire
Kimberly Burnham * Shareef Abdur – Rasheed
Ashok K. Bhargava * Elizabeth Castillo * Swapna Behera
Tezmin Ition Tsai * William S. Peters, Sr.

The Year of the Poet VI
June 2019

Featured Poets
Kate Gaudi Puwiekszone * Sahaj Sabharwal
Iwu Jeff * Mohamed Abdel Aziz Shmeis

Arctic
Circumpolar

The Poetry Posse 2019

Gail Weston Shazor * Albert Carrasco * Hülya N. Yılmaz
Jackie Davis Allen * Caroline Nazareno * Eliza Segiet
Alicja Maria Kubeska * Teresa E. Gallion * Joe Paire
Kimberly Burnham * Shareef Abdur – Rasheed
Ashok K. Bhargava * Elizabeth Castillo * Swapna Behera
Tezmin Ition Tsai * William S. Peters, Sr.

The Year of the Poet VI

Featured Poets
Saadeddin Shahin * Andy Scott
Fabrello Sholu * Alok Kumar Ray

The Horn of Africa

Ethiopia   Djibouti

Somalia   Eritrea

The Poetry Posse 2019

Gail Weston Shazor * Albert Carrasco * Hülya N. Yılmaz
Jackie Davis Allen * Caroline Nazareno * Eliza Segiet
Alicja Maria Kubeska * Teresa E. Gallion * Joe Paire
Kimberly Burnham * Shareef Abdur – Rasheed
Ashok K. Bhargava * Elizabeth Castillo * Swapna Behera
Tezmin Ition Tsai * William S. Peters, Sr.

The Year of the Poet VI
August 2019

Featured Poets
Shola Balogun * Bharati Nayak
Monalisa Dash Dwibedy * Mbizo Chirasha

Coexist

Southwest Asia

The Poetry Posse 2019

Gail Weston Shazor * Albert Carrasco * Hülya N. Yılmaz
Jackie Davis Allen * Caroline Nazareno * Eliza Segiet
Alicja Maria Kubeska * Teresa E. Gallion * Joe Paire
Kimberly Burnham * Shareef Abdur – Rasheed
Ashok K. Bhargava * Elizabeth Castillo * Swapna Behera
Tezmin Ition Tsai * William S. Peters, Sr.

Now Available

www.innerchildpress.com/the-year-of-the-poet

The Year of the Poet VI
September 2019
Featured Poets
Elena Liliana Popescu * Gobinda Biswas
Iram Fatima 'Ashi' * Joseph S. Spence, Sr.

The Caucasus
The Poetry Posse 2019

Gail Weston Shazor * Albert Carrasco * Hülya N. Yılmaz
Jackie Davis Allen * Caroline Nazareno * Eliza Segiet
Alicja Maria Kuberska * Teresa E. Gallion * Joe Paire
Kimberly Burnham * Shareef Abdur – Rasheed
Ashok K. Bhargava * Elizabeth Castillo * Swapna Behera
Tezmin Ition Tsai * William S. Peters. Sr.

The Year of the Poet VI
October 2019
Featured Poets
Ngozi Olivia Osuoha * Denisa Kondic
Parkhuri Sinha * Christena AV Williams

The Nile Valley
The Poetry Posse 2019

Gail Weston Shazor * Albert Carrasco * Hülya N. Yılmaz
Jackie Davis Allen * Caroline Nazareno * Eliza Segiet
Alicja Maria Kuberska * Teresa E. Gallion * Joe Paire
Kimberly Burnham * Shareef Abdur – Rasheed
Ashok K. Bhargava * Elizabeth Castillo * Swapna Behera
Tezmin Ition Tsai * William S. Peters. Sr.

The Year of the Poet VI
November 2019
Featured Poets
Rozalia Aleksandrova * Gobindu Ganga
Smruti Ranjan Mohanty * Sofia Skleida

Northern Asia
The Poetry Posse 2019

Gail Weston Shazor * Albert Carrasco * Hülya N. Yılmaz
Jackie Davis Allen * Caroline Nazareno * Eliza Segiet
Alicja Maria Kuberska * Teresa E. Gallion * Joe Paire
Kimberly Burnham * Shareef Abdur – Rasheed
Ashok K. Bhargava * Elizabeth Castillo * Swapna Behera
Tezmin Ition Tsai * William S. Peters. Sr.

The Year of the Poet VI
December 2019
Featured Poets
Robin Karim (Kachner) * Sujata Paul
Bharat Nayak * Kapardeli Eftichia

Oceania
The Poetry Posse 2019

Gail Weston Shazor * Albert Carrasco * Hülya N. Yılmaz
Jackie Davis Allen * Caroline Nazareno * Eliza Segiet
Alicja Maria Kuberska * Teresa E. Gallion * Joe Paire
Kimberly Burnham * Shareef Abdur – Rasheed
Ashok K. Bhargava * Elizabeth Castillo * Swapna Behera
Tezmin Ition Tsai * William S. Peters. Sr.

Now Available

www.innerchildpress.com/the-year-of-the-poet

The Year of the Poet VII
January 2020

Featured Poets
B S Tyagi * Ashok Chakravarthy Tholana
Andy Scott * Anwer Ghani

1901 Jean Henry Dunant and Frédéric Passy

The Year of Peace
Celebrating past Nobel Peace Prize Recipients

The Poetry Posse 2020
Gail Weston Shazor * Albert Carasico * Hülya N. Yılmaz
Jackie Davis Allen * Caroline Nazareno * Eliza Segiet
Alicja Maria Kuberska * Teresa E. Gallion * Joe Paire
Kimberly Burnham * Shareef Abdur – Rasheed
Ashok K. Bhargava * Elizabeth Castillo * Swapna Behera
Tezmin Ition Tsai * William S. Peters, Sr.

The Year of the Poet VII
February 2020

Featured Poets
Jennifer Ades * Martina Reisz Newberry
Ibrahim Honjo * Claudia Piccinno

Henri La Fontaine ~ 1913

The Year of Peace
Celebrating past Nobel Peace Prize Recipients

The Poetry Posse 2020
Gail Weston Shazor * Albert Carasico * Hülya N. Yılmaz
Jackie Davis Allen * Caroline Nazareno * Eliza Segiet
Alicja Maria Kuberska * Teresa E. Gallion * Joe Paire
Kimberly Burnham * Shareef Abdur – Rasheed
Ashok K. Bhargava * Elizabeth Castillo * Swapna Behera
Tezmin Ition Tsai * William S. Peters, Sr.

The Year of the Poet VII
March 2020

Featured Poets
Aziz Mountassir * Krishna Paraisa
Hannie Rouweler * Rozalia Aleksandrova

Aristide Briand ~ 1926 ~ Gustav Stresemann

The Year of Peace
Celebrating past Nobel Peace Prize Recipients

The Poetry Posse 2020
Gail Weston Shazor * Albert Carasico * Hülya N. Yılmaz
Jackie Davis Allen * Caroline Nazareno * Eliza Segiet
Alicja Maria Kuberska * Teresa E. Gallion * Joe Paire
Kimberly Burnham * Shareef Abdur – Rasheed
Ashok K. Bhargava * Elizabeth Castillo * Swapna Behera
Tezmin Ition Tsai * William S. Peters, Sr.

The Year of the Poet VII
April 2020

Featured Poets
Rohini Behera * Mircea Dan Duta
Monalisa Dash Dwibedy * NilavroNill Shoovro

Carlos Saavedra Lamas ~ 1936

The Year of Peace
Celebrating past Nobel Peace Prize Recipients

The Poetry Posse 2020
Gail Weston Shazor * Albert Carasico * Hülya N. Yılmaz
Jackie Davis Allen * Caroline Nazareno * Eliza Segiet
Alicja Maria Kuberska * Teresa E. Gallion * Joe Paire
Kimberly Burnham * Shareef Abdur – Rasheed
Ashok K. Bhargava * Elizabeth Castillo * Swapna Behera
Tezmin Ition Tsai * William S. Peters, Sr.

Now Available

www.innerchildpress.com/the-year-of-the-poet

The Year of the Poet VII
May 2020

Featured Poets
Alok Kumar Ray * Eden S. Trinidad
Franco Barbato * Izabela Zubko

Ralph Bunche ~ 1950

The Year of Peace
Celebrating past Nobel Peace Prize Recipients

The Poetry Posse 2020
Gail Weston Shazor * Albert Carasco * Hülya N. Yılmaz
Jackie Davis Allen * Caroline Nazareno * Eliza Segiet
Alicja Maria Kubeska * Teresa E. Gallion * Joe Paire
Kimberly Burnham * Shareef Abdur – Rasheed
Ashok K. Bhargava * Elizabeth Castillo * Swapna Behera
Tezmin Ition Tsai * William S. Peters, Sr.

The Year of the Poet VII
June 2020

Featured Poets
Eftichia Kapardeli * Metin Cengiz
Hussein Habasch * Kosh K Mathew

Albert John Lutuli ~ 1960

The Year of Peace
Celebrating past Nobel Peace Prize Recipients

The Poetry Posse 2020
Gail Weston Shazor * Albert Carasco * Hülya N. Yılmaz
Jackie Davis Allen * Caroline Nazareno * Eliza Segiet
Alicja Maria Kubeska * Teresa E. Gallion * Joe Paire
Kimberly Burnham * Shareef Abdur – Rasheed
Ashok K. Bhargava * Elizabeth Castillo * Swapna Behera
Tezmin Ition Tsai * William S. Peters, Sr.

The Year of the Poet VII
July 2020

Featured Poets
Mykola Martyniuk * Orbindu Ganga
Roula Pollard * Karn Praktisha

Norman Ernest Borlaug ~ 1970

The Year of Peace
Celebrating past Nobel Peace Prize Recipients

The Poetry Posse 2020
Gail Weston Shazor * Albert Carasco * Hülya N. Yılmaz
Jackie Davis Allen * Caroline Nazareno * Eliza Segiet
Alicja Maria Kubeska * Teresa E. Gallion * Joe Paire
Kimberly Burnham * Shareef Abdur – Rasheed
Ashok K. Bhargava * Elizabeth Castillo * Swapna Behera
Tezmin Ition Tsai * William S. Peters, Sr.

Now Available

www.innerchildpress.com/the-year-of-the-poet

and there is much, much more !

visit . . .

www.innerchildpress.com/antho
logies-sales-special.php

Also check out our Authors and
all the wonderful Books
Available at :

www.innerchildpress.com/autho
rs-pages

World Healing World Peace
2020

Poets for Humanity

Now Available

www.worldhealingworldpeacepoetry.com

INNER CHILD PRESS

WORLD HEALING WORLD PEACE

2018

A Poetry Anthology for Humanity

Now Available

www.worldhealingworldpeacepoetry.com

I support World Healing World Peace

www.worldhealingworldpeacepoetry.com

World Healing World Peace

i am a believer!

World Healing World Peace

2012, 2014, 2016, 2018, 2020

Now Available

www.worldhealingworldpeacepoetry.com

213

Inner Child Press International

'building bridges of cultural understanding'

Meet our Cultural Ambassadors

Fahredin Shehu
Director of Cultural

Faleha Hassan
Iraq – USA

Elizabeth E. Castillo
Philippines

Antoinette Coleman
Chicago
Midwest USA

Ananda Nepali
Nepal – East
Northern India

Kimberly Burnham
Pacific Northwest
USA

Alicja Kuberska
Poland
Eastern Europe

Swapna Behera
India
Southeast Asia

Kolade O. Freedom
Nigeria
West Africa

Monsif Beroual
Morocco
Northern Africa

Ashok K. Bhargava
Canada

Tzemin Ition Tsai
Republic of China
Greater China

Alicia M. Ramírez
Mexico
Central America

Christena AV Williams
Jamaica
Caribbean

Louise Hudon
Eastern Canada

Aziz Mountassir
Morocco
Northern Africa

Shareef Abdur-Rasheed
Southeastern USA

Laure Charazac
France
Western Europe

Mohammad Ikhal Harb
Lebanon
Middle East

**Mohamed Abdel
Aziz Shmeis**
Egypt
Middle East

Hilary Mainga
Kenya
Eastern Africa

Josephus R. Johnson
Liberia

www.innerchildpress.com

This Anthological Publication
is underwritten solely by

Inner Child Press International

Inner Child Press is a Publishing Company Founded and Operated by Writers. Our personal publishing experiences provides us an intimate understanding of the sometimes daunting challenges Writers, New and Seasoned may face in the Business of Publishing and Marketing their Creative "Written Work".

For more Information

Inner Child Press International

www.innerchildpress.com

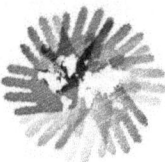

'building bridges of cultural understanding'

202 Wiltree Court, State College, Pennsylvania 16801

www.innerchildpress.com

~ fini ~

www.ingramcontent.com/pod-product-compliance
Lightning Source LLC
LaVergne TN
LVHW011152080426
835508LV00007B/366